Good BASIC P
with the BBC M

Macmillan Microcomputer Books

General Editor: Ian Birnbaum (General Adviser (Microelectronics in Education), Education Department, Humberside County Council)

Advanced Graphics with the Acorn Electron
  Ian O. Angell and Brian J. Jones
Advanced Graphics with the BBC Model B Microcomputer
  Ian O. Angell and Brian J. Jones
Interfacing the BBC Microcomputer
  Brian Bannister and Michael Whitehead
Assembly Language Programming for the Acorn Electron
  Ian Birnbaum
Assembly Language Programming for the BBC Microcomputer (second edition)
  Ian Birnbaum
Using Your Home Computer (Practical Projects for the Micro Owner)
  Garth W. P. Davies
Microchild — Learning through LOGO
  Serafim Gascoigne
A Science Teacher's Companion to the BBC Microcomputer
  Philip Hawthorne
Beginning BASIC with the ZX Spectrum
  Judith Miller
Using Sound and Speech on the BBC Microcomputer
  Martin Phillips
File Handling on the BBC Microcomputer
  Brian J. Townsend
Good BASIC Programming with the BBC Microcomputer
  Margaret White

Other Books of Related Interest

Advanced Graphics with the IBM Personal Computer
  Ian O. Angell
Advanced Graphics with the Sinclair ZX Spectrum
  Ian O. Angell and Brian J. Jones
Using CP/M
  Peter Gosling
Programming in Z80 Assembly Language
  Roger Hutty
Computer Literacy — A Beginners' Guide
  Vincent Walsh

Good BASIC Programming with the BBC Microcomputer

Margaret A. White

MACMILLAN

First published 1985

Published by
Higher and Further Education Division
MACMILLAN PUBLISHERS LTD
Houndmills, Basingstoke, Hampshire RG21 2XS
and London
Companies and representatives
throughout the world

Printed in Great Britain by Camelot Press, Southampton

British Library Cataloguing in Publication Data
White, M.A.
   Good Basic programming with the BBC Microcomputer.
   —(Macmillan microcomputer books)
   1. BBC Microcomputer—Programming   2. Basic
   (Computer program language)
   I. Title
   001.64′24   QA76.8.B35

   ISBN 0–333–36704–9

Contents

Preface

There are many books written about the BBC microcomputer and even more about BASIC itself.

This book is intended primarily for the programmer who wants to produce programs for the BBC micro in a professional manner. However, there is also plenty here to interest anyone who uses a microcomputer, BBC or otherwise: the professional programmer, the novice programmer, the beginner, the micro user (pupil, student, teacher, child, parent, businessman, clerk etc.), or the micro manager (teacher, child, parent, businessman, department manager etc.), and particularly the micro owner who is an all-in-one programmer, user and manager!

The principles discussed in this book contribute to the production of a ´good´ program according to my criteria, and although you will probably dispute some points I hope there are others with which you agree.

The ideas discussed are application independent, that is, they are equally applicable to software produced for games, education, business, private use etc.

There is no need to have access to a micro when reading this book (although this would, of course, be an advantage). Since the book contains no operating instructions for the BBC microcomputer, if you do want to experiment and you have not used the micro before, you will need to find out how to operate it from the User Guide or elsewhere. Many of the examples shown will also work on micros other than the BBC Model B. An indication is given of those features of the Extended Version of BASIC that are discussed but are not generally available on other micros.

The first chapter attempts to define a good program and to give some hints about its production, while chapter 2 is concerned with some of the simpler processes that can be carried out on a micro (mainly for the benefit of novices).

Chapters 3 to 7 deal with programming itself, and should be of interest to all programmers from beginner to expert. Chapter 8 discusses the testing of programs from the point of view of the programmer, the user and the manager. The handling of data is dealt with in chapter 9 - from the keyboard, the program, and to and from cassette and disk. Chapter 10 is concerned with particular features of the BBC micro - graphics, sound and functions.

After discussion of implementation and review in chapter 11, the final chapter attempts to highlight some of the more important points from the text.

I hope you find the book useful. Comments from readers will be most welcome.

Margaret White

1 Introduction and Program Production

1.1 What is a Good Program?

The answer to the question posed by this section will depend on your relationship to your microcomputer. If you are a manager the answer might be "A program that does what I want it to do". If you are a user the answer could be "One that´s nice and easy to use" (that is, user-friendly!). Should you be a programmer the answer might be "One that works", and if you are already a good programmer you will probably add "and in six month´s time when you ask me to change it, this should not be too difficult".

So we have to produce a program that

(a) does what the manager wants
(b) is easy to use
(c) works (as far as the programmer is concerned)
(d) is easy to change.

Note that (c) is the only criterion directly related to writing the program in BASIC.

Doing what the manager wants and working to the programmer´s satisfaction are not necessarily the same thing!

At this point it is worth considering the stages required in the production of a program. They are

> specification
> program design
> coding
> testing
> implementation
> review.

Specification is a description of the processing, in plain English,to be carried out by the program. For example, a program to check mental arithmetic is such a broad specification that it must be broken down into more detailed stages before a useful program can be produced or, if a program exists already, before a manager can evaluate the usefulness of the

program. Although a manager should always experiment
with a program he is evaluating, comprehensive
specifications ought nevertheless to be available.

A program to check mental arithmetic might have the
following stipulations

(1) it should involve no more than four factors, each
of which is to have no more than two digits
(2) only addition and subtraction are to be considered
(3) each question should remain on the screen for 20
seconds.

The requirements are given here in sufficient detail
for a programmer to start work and for a manager to
make an evaluation.

Program design is a description of the processing,
in logical terms, to be carried out by the program. The
programmer must take the detailed specification and
convert it into logical processes which the computer
can carry out. This topic will be covered in detail in
chapter 3.

Coding is the translation of the program design into
the computer language used, in this case BBC
BASIC. This topic is covered in detail throughout the
text, particularly in chapters 4, 5 and 7.

Testing is the checking of two aspects - that the
coding matches the design and that it also meets the
specification. Testing is considered in detail in
chapter 8.

Implementation is the introduction of the program
into the application area, such as a classroom, office
or home.

Review is the evaluation of the program's
performance.

The specification, implementation and review stages,
if done well, will ensure that the program does what
the manager wants and is easy to use. The design,
coding and testing stages, if done well, will ensure
that all criteria are met (that is, the program will
look good to the manager, the user and the programmer).

1.2 Documentation

To many programmers, documentation is a dirty word. It
is too often considered only after the program is
finished, and its production is considered to be a
boring job. In instances where documentation was
previously skimpy and insufficient, many managers often
opt for the opposite extreme and require the production
of reams of paper which no-one wants to read and
everyone finds difficult to understand. There has to be
a balance.

The documentation of the specification must enable the programmer to produce what is required and also enable a manager to initially evaluate a program before experimenting with it himself. For example, a diet program (to check daily consumption of fat, vitamins, carbohydrates etc.) ought to specify whether it caters for both men and women, what age range it covers etc. The documentation produced for program design is not something to be drawn up after the program is written, it is a necessary part of the design process. Within the program code, as many opportunities as possible should be taken to make the program more understandable, such as translating the program design into code in a standard fashion and using meaningful names for data (grosspay, netpay, interestrate, deposit, multiplier etc.). The number of actual comments or remarks in the program can then be minimised.

Documenting the results of tests has a two-fold benefit: it ensures that the quality of the testing data can be examined and it provides a base for testing when amendments are made to the program. Documenting the effects of implementation ensures that urgent corrections can be distinguished from desirable alterations. Documenting comments made by the manager, the user and the programmer during review ensures that due care is taken before amendments are made.

1.3 Variables (Names)

Programs are concerned with processing data and, in order to process data, we must store each item (such as a number or a person´s name) in a separate store. Each store will have a name which we can choose. In a payroll program, for instance, we might use the names

    employeename
    hours
    hourlyrate
    bonus
    tax
    ni

to store the appropriate figures for an employee, and use the names

    grosspay
    netpay

when we want to calculate gross and net pay.

These eight names are permissible in a BASIC program on the BBC micro. There are four rules to which all names must conform. They are

1. There must be no spaces in the middle of a variable name (net pay is not allowed).
2. All variable names must begin with a letter (2fig is not allowed).
3. The remaining characters in the name can be letters, digits or underlines (big! is not allowed). Warning: note that netpay and net_pay are not the same store.
4. Variable names should not begin with BASIC keywords (that is, IF TO etc.). There are more than 100 of these! However, BASIC keywords have to be written in upper case, so if you always use lower case for your variable names you do not have to worry. Using lower case also means that the variable name is distinguished from the keywords and thus the program is easier to read. Lower case names will be used throughout this text.

1.4 Variables (Types)

Having chosen the names for the variables, we now have to decide the kind of data we wish to store in each variable (for example, a number, a person's name etc.).

Numbers can be of two types, real or integer. A real number is one that can have decimal places (for example, 6.8, 45.21345, -9.0). An integer number is a whole number (for example, 6, 54, -9).

Data such as a person's name (that is, something which is not numeric) is held as a "string".

If we want to hold an integer number we should put a % after the name to indicate that this store will hold only integer values. (Integer arithmetic is much easier and thus faster than real arithmetic.) If we want to hold a string we should put a $ after the name to indicate that this store will hold only a string.

In our payroll program for instance, we would use the names (assuming that we know hourlyrate and bonus can be only whole numbers - probably pence)

```
employeename$
hours
hourlyrate%
bonus%
tax
ni
```

to store the appropriate figures for an employee, and use the names

    grosspay
    netpay

when we want to calculate gross and net pay.

    I try to use the variable names in my program design and thus make the production of the program code and its subsequent understanding easier.

    For a large program it is also a good idea to keep a list which gives the names and their uses in the program. For example

Name	Use
employeename$	read in and print out name
hours	read in number of hours worked for calculation
hourlyrate%	read in hourlyrate for calculation
bonus%	read in bonus for calculation
tax	store calculated tax
ni	store calculated ni
grosspay	store calculated grosspay
netpay	store calculated netpay

    If you are a novice programmer or user or manager, you may prefer to leave the next section on dimensioned variables until after you have read chapter 2. It is included here for completeness.

1.5 Dimensioned Variables (Arrays)

The variables that we discussed in sections 1.3 and 1.4 are really simple variables, that is, there is only one store with a particular name. In many programs, however, we are interested in sets of data; for example, a set of football results. Suppose we wish to store the following table

Team	Colour	Played	Won	Drawn	Lost	Goals for	Goals against	Av.
1	RED	2	1	1	0	3	1	1.5
2	GREEN	1	0	0	1	0	2	0
3	YELLOW	1	0	1	0	1	1	1
4	BLACK	0	0	0	0	0	0	0

For each team we need to store the colour in a string, the numbers of games played, won, drawn and lost, and the numbers of goals for and against in integers, and the average in a real variable.

If we want to store a colour as a string we might choose the name

```
colour$
```

so if we have four teams we must define an array at the beginning of our program as, for example

```
20 DIM colour$(4)
```

This means that we have set up four stores whose names are

```
colour$(1),colour$(2),colour$(3) and colour$(4)
```

Similarly for the average we must define an array at the beginning of our program as, for example

```
30 DIM average(4)
```

The above two arrays each have four "rows" corresponding to the four "rows" in the table. To store the integer values we need four "rows" each of six "columns", since there are six integer values to store for each "row". In this case we must define an array having four "rows" and six "columns" at the beginning of our program as, for example

```
40 DIM matchandgoal%(4,6)
```

Note that the terms "row" and "column" are not always used as horizontal and vertical indicators as I have shown here, so be careful when looking at other texts or programs.

This array has 24 elements, and the information for the first team would be stored in

```
matchandgoal%(1,1)
matchandgoal%(1,2)
matchandgoal%(1,3)
matchandgoal%(1,4)
matchandgoal%(1,5)
matchandgoal%(1,6).
```

The information for the second team would be stored in

```
matchandgoal%(2,1)
matchandgoal%(2,2)
matchandgoal%(2,3)
matchandgoal%(2,4)
matchandgoal%(2,5)
matchandgoal%(2,6) and so on,
```

the last element being matchandgoal%(4,6) to store the
goals against for the last team. This is known as a
two-dimensional array.

The BBC microcomputer allows arrays to have as many
dimensions as you wish, provided that   there   is
sufficient memory.
Note that DIM colour$(4) actually sets up five stores
since the first element is colour$(0). Similarly, DIM
matchandgoal%(4,6) actually sets up thirty-five stores
(5x7). I find counting from one easier to understand
and in some cases use element zero for special
purposes. However, to reduce program size it may be
necessary to count from zero rather than one.

1.6 Summary
In this chapter I have attempted to define a "good"
program and also to give some hints on the use of
documentation and the choosing of variable names and
types before program design and coding starts. However,
particularly during design, it may be found necessary
to add to the variable list.

2 Simple Coding in BASIC

2.1 Introduction

In many respects this chapter should come after chapter 3, since program design should be thoroughly completed before coding begins. However, in practice, if you have no knowledge of the kind of processing a computer can do or the language features available to you, it can be difficult to understand the important principles of program design. So this chapter is really to give novices an idea of some of the simpler processes that can be carried out in BBC BASIC. If you already have an elementary knowledge of BASIC or a good knowledge of some other language you might prefer to skip this chapter and return to it after you have read chapter 3. The statements discussed will be INPUT, PRINT, REM, END, LET, READ, DATA and CLS.

2.2 Example Program

```
10 REM THIS IS CHAPTER 2.2 EXAMPLE
20 INPUT "What is your name , please ",name$
30 PRINT "Hello ";name$
40 END
```

This four-line program contains four statements - REM, INPUT, PRINT, END. We will look at them in turn in just a moment.

   If we execute (RUN) the program

      What is your name , please ?

will appear on the screen. If we type in JAMES and press the RETURN key, then

      Hello JAMES

will appear on the screen.

   We will now look at these four statements (and a few others) in more detail. At this stage all we need to note is that the line numbers 10, 20, 30, 40 above merely indicate the order in which these statements are to be executed.

8

2.3 The INPUT Statement
The INPUT statement is used to put information into the
computer via the keyboard. For example

```
10 INPUT age%
20 INPUT name$
30 INPUT numberofhours
```

will store an integer number into age%, a string into
name$ and a real number into numberofhours.
    Normally we would precede the variable name with a
message, otherwise the user may not understand what
information is required. For example

```
10 INPUT "How old are you",age%
20 INPUT "What is your name",name$
30 INPUT "Numberofhours = "numberofhours
```
In this last example notice that there is no comma
between the message and the variable name. In this case
a ? is not printed after the message.
    If you want to input several values immediately one
after the other, you can combine them in one INPUT
statement. For example

```
50 INPUT "First name = " fname$ "Second name = " sname$
```

will wait for a string to be entered for fname$ and
then request a string for sname$.

```
60 INPUT "Put in 2 numbers",fno,sno
```

will print the message and wait for two numbers which
must be separated either by a comma or the RETURN key.

2.4 The PRINT Statement
The PRINT statement is used to pass information from
the computer to the user on the screen. It is used to
print "messages" or the contents of variables, or a
combination of both. For example

```
40 PRINT "THIS PROGRAM CALCULATES COMPCUND INTEREST"
60 PRINT numberofaliensleft%
70 PRINT rate * 0.01 * principal
80 PRINT "Number of arrows in bull = "; bulla, "Misses
= "; missa
90 PRINT name$
```

Anything enclosed in inverted commas is treated as a
message and printed. So for line 40 the words THIS
PROGRAM CALCULATES COMPOUND INTEREST will appear on the

screen.

   Anything not enclosed in inverted commas is treated
as a character string or numeric expression, as
appropriate, and the result is calculated and printed.
So for line 60 the contents of numberofaliensleft% will
be printed, and for line 70 the contents of rate and
principal and the constant 0.01 will be multiplied
together and the result printed.

   Line 80 illustrates the two techniques used to print
a single line of information of words and figures. Line
90 illustrates the printing of a character string, in
this case the contents of name$. The statement

20 PRINT

gives a blank line.

   A semi-colon after an item ensures that the next
item is printed on the same line and immediately
folowing the previous item. Commas between items ensure
that they are printed in adjacent "fields". The width
is by default 10 characters wide but it can be changed.
Numbers can be printed out in several different layouts
by changing the overall field with, the total number of
figures printed and the number of decimal places
(according to the value in the variable @%). However,
explanation of this facility will be found outside this
text.

2.5 The REM Statement

The REM statement is used to store information about
the program for the benefit of the programmer. REM
statements do make the program slower but enough REMs
must be included to identify the program and its major
components. When a program is RUN, anything after REM
on a line is ignored and so the information is not
shown to the user. For example

10 REM THIS PROGRAM CALCULATES SIMPLE INTEREST
50 REM THIS PROCEDURE DRAWS A CIRCLE

   Some programmers list all variables and their uses
by REM statements at the beginning of the program. This
is a good idea, but where the number of variables is
large it is probably preferable to keep a separate list
which is filed away with an up-to-date program listing
(and program design) for reference.

REM need not be the only statement on the line, but anything after the word REM is taken as comment. For example

20500 PRINT "Number of hits is " ; nhits : REM End of first round

Note that the colon is used to separate the PRINT statement from the REM statement.

2.6 The END Statement
The END statement is used to indicate the logical end of the program, that is, all processing is complete. In simple programs END is not mandatory. Thus

```
10 REM THIS IS CHAPTER 2.5 EXAMPLE
20 INPUT "What is your name , please ",name$
30 PRINT "Hello ";name$
```

works just the same as the original program with 40 END included. However, if data is included at the physical end of the program, it is easier to distinguish the program from its data if there is an END in between and, if subroutines, procedures or functions are included at the physical end, END must be used to show the logical end. So personally I always put END at the logical end whether it is required or not.
    In some situations (particularly when handling errors) more than one logical end may be needed. For instance

```
12000 ...
12100 PRINT "TIME LIMIT EXCEEDED"
12200 END
12300 PRINT "I WON!"
12400 END
12500 PRINT "YOU WON = WELL DONE!!!"
12600 END
```

Here the program may finish processing at line 12200, 12400 or 12600. Do not worry at this stage about how we reached 12100, 12300 or 12500.

2.7 The LET (Assignment) Statement
The LET or assignment statement is used to replace the contents of a variable, that is, to assign a value to a variable.
    We already know that there are three types of variables - integer, real and string - and therefore we

can use the assignment statement to store an integer
value, real value or string value as appropriate. For
example

```
10 LET total% = 0
20 LET percent = 2.5
30 LET totpercent = 0
40 LET name$ = "SMITH"
```

In these examples total% and totpercent become equal to
zero, percent becomes 2.5 and name$ becomes SMITH.
    The value after = should be consistent with the
variable before = (that is, numeric or string). It is
evaluated and then converted to the appropriate type
for assignment. For instance 70 stock% = 3.5 will put 3
into stock%.
    Note that the string of characters to be placed in a
string variable must be enclosed in inverted commas.
    The value after = can be a constant as in the
examples above, or a variable name, or an expression.
    Examples using variable names are

```
10 LET total% = wktotal%
20 LET percent = currentrate
40 LET name$ = oldname$
```

In these examples the contents of the variable
preceding = have been changed and are equal to the
contents of the variable after the =. The variable
after the = is unchanged.
    An example using expressions is

```
10 LET total% = total% + thisfig%
```

In this example the contents of tctal% and thisfig% are
added together and the result placed in total%,
thisfig% being unchanged. Another such example is

```
20 LET percent = currentrate * 0.01
```

In this example the contents of currentrate and the
constant 0.01 are multiplied together and the result
placed in percent, currentrate being unchanged. Yet
another example is

```
40 LET name$ = firstname$ + " " + secondname$
```

In this example the contents of firstname$, the
constant "space" and the contents of secondname$ are
concatenated (strung) together and the result placed in
name$, firstname$ and secondname$ being unchanged.

Numeric variables can be joined by a combination of
operators,   some   of   which   are   +   (addition),   -
(subtraction), * (multiplication), / (division)   or   ^
(raise to the power). Brackets may be used to force
precedence (or for readability) as in mathematics. For
example

750 LET answer = (num1 + num2) * (num3 / num4)

This   means   add the contents of num1 and num2 together
to give an intermediate result one, divide the contents
of num3 by the contents of num4 to give an intermediate
result   two,   multiply   intermediate   result   one   by
intermediate result two and put the result into answer.
The   two operators DIV and MOD can be used to carry out
integer division.
    DIV gives the whole number (integer) quotient from a
division. MOD gives the whole number (integer)
remainder from a division. For example

910 LET quot% = fno% DIV secno%
920 LET remn% = fno% MOD secno%

Assuming that fno% contains 14 and secno% contains 5,
quot% will contain 2 and remn% will contain 4.
    All numbers used in the calculation of the operators
DIV and MOD are first converted to truncated integers.
For instance

910 LET quot = fno DIV secno
920 LET remn = fno MOD secno

Assuming that fno contains 14.6 and secno contains 5.1,
quot will contain 2.0 and remn will contain 4.0.
    The   word   LET   is optional. If you are a novice you
may find it useful to include it to remind yourself
that you are replacing the contents of the variable
name after LET. However, most programmers omit LET and,
since I do not think that LET makes the program any
more understandable, I shall omit it from now on. The
above example then becomes

910 quot = fno DIV secno
920 remn = fno MOD secno

2.8 The READ and DATA Statements
There are many ways of entering data into a program,
the INPUT statement above being one such method. Use of

the READ and DATA statements is a second method. For
example

```
 5 REM THIS IS CHAPTER 2.8 EXAMPLE
10 READ byear
20 READ nyear
30 age1 = nyear - byear
40 age2 = age1 - 1
50 PRINT "You are either " ; age2 ; " or " ; age1 ;
   " years of age"
60 END
100 DATA 1902,1984
```

When the program is run the data pointer is set at
the first DATA statement, in this case line 100, and
each time a READ statement is executed an item of data
is taken from the data list and deposited in the
variable specified in the READ statement. In this case
1902 is transferred to byear and 1984 to nyear. Further
examples of this technique and other methods of data
handling are dealt with in chapter 9.

2.9 The CLS Statement
It is often desirable to clear the screen before
producing any output. This is achieved by using the CLS
statement. For instance

```
40 CLS
```

The output from the program that follows will appear at
the top of the screen. For example

```
 5 REM THIS IS CHAPTER 2.9 EXAMPLE
10 READ byear
20 READ nyear
30 age1 = nyear - byear
40 age2 = age1 - 1
45 CLS
50 PRINT "You are either " ; age2 ; " or " ; age1 ;
   " years of age"
60 END
100 DATA 1902,1984
```

Further screen techniques are discussed in chapter
10.

2.10 Summary
The statements INPUT, PRINT, END, LET, READ and CLS are
all examples of action statements, that is, we are

asking the computer to do something such as request data, display information, finish processing, perform a calculation, get data or clear the screen.

Now that we have some idea of the simpler processes that the computer can carry out, we should be able to put them into a logical order (see chapter 3) and translate the design into a good program (see chapters 4, 5 and 7). The complete program example in chapter 6 will not contain any action instructions other than the ones discussed here.

3 Program Design

3.1 Introduction

In this chapter I want to show you how I would design a program for any computer, a micro, a mini or a mainframe. Thus, the technique is independent of machine and programming language. It is based on the principles of top-down design (breaking a program down into more and more detail), but there are probably as many versions of top-down design as there are books on the subject - so here is my version!

The purpose of program design is to form a logical description of the processing required by the computer (always bearing the user in mind!) without getting bogged down in the details of the program instructions necessary to carry it out. This logical description is more likely to be correct, more understandable and easier to update if we restrict ourselves when designing to "constructs" called sequences, selections and iterations. Fundamentally, a sequence represents the order in which we carry things out, a selection (decision) indicates that a choice between several alternatives is made, and an iteration (loop) indicates that we wish to repeat some process.

However, before we can start designing we must have some idea of the elementary actions which can be carried out on our computer, even if we do not know exactly how to code them. For instance, in chapter 2, we saw that it is possible on the BBC micro to enter numbers or strings at the keyboard, to print a string or the contents of a store on the screen, to change the contents of a store using addition, subtraction etc., and so on. The instructions shown in chapter 2 are sufficient to illustrate the design technique and to give a complete design and coding example in chapter 6. The instructions such as

```
enter a number from the keyboard
print count
print "I WON"
add 1 to count
```

are called elementary actions (that is, they do nct need to be described any further) and they require immediate action.

Even though we are using one method of top-down design, the logic can be represented in words (figure 3.1a) or a diagram (figure 3.1b) or by flowchart (figure 3.1c). I always use (a) or (b), never (c). I

16

have included flowcharts in the subsequent figures only to illustrate the method and do not recommend their use except for extremely small BASIC programs or occasionally for assembly language routines.

3.2 Sequence

A sequence represents a series of processes which are carried out in order. For instance a sequence of three elementary actions would be represented as shown in figure 3.1. In this example we wish to carry out the elementary actions of entering a name at the keyboard, printing hello and the person´s name, and finishing the program.

(a)   1.1 Ask for user´s name
        1.2 Print Hello and user´s name
        1.3 Finish

        END

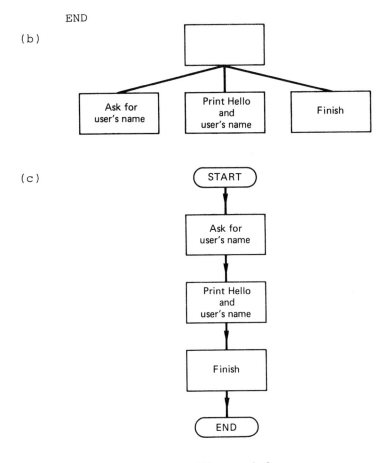

Figure 3.1

This simple example is a sequence of elementary actions, but any program can be regarded as a sequence which is gradually broken down into sequences, selections and iterations.

3.3 Selection
A selection consists of choosing one of a number of alternatives. There are several "types" of selections - I have found four to be sufficient. The selection is enclosed between the words IF and ENDIF or CASE and ENDCASE, as will be seen below.

Type 1
In this first type we want to carry out some process only if a condition is true. If the condition is false, then we wish to do nothing. In either event we would then proceed to the next process in the sequence.

In the example of figure 3.2 we wish to carry out the elementary action of printing the word PASS if the mark is larger than 50.

(a)   2.0 IF mark larger than 50
        2.1 THEN
        2.2   PRINT "PASS"
        2.3 ENDIF

(b)

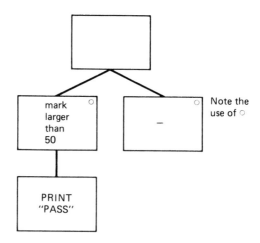

(c)

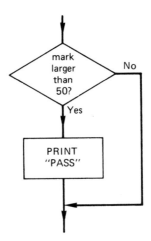

Figure 3.2

Type 2

In this second type we want to carry out a particular process if the condition is true. If the condition is false we wish to carry out an alternative process (that is, we are choosing 1 from 2). In either event we would then proceed to the next process in the sequence.

In the example of figure 3.3 we wish to carry out the elementary action of printing the word PASS if the mark is larger than 50 and printing the word FAIL if the mark is not larger than 50.

(a)   3.0 IF mark larger than 50
        3.1 THEN
        3.2   PRINT "PASS"
        3.3 ELSE
        3.4   PRINT "FAIL"
        3.5 ENDIF

(b)

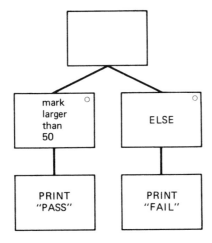

(c)

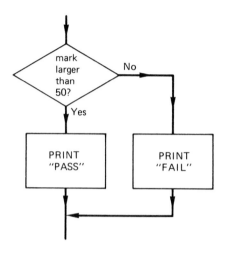

Figure 3.3

Type 3
In this third type we want to carry out a process if
the first condition is true. If the first condition is
false we wish to carry out a further condition test,
with one process to carry out if it is true and an
alternative if it is false (that is, we are choosing 1
from 3). In any event we would then proceed to the next
process in the sequence.

In the example of figure 3.4 we wish to carry out
the elementary action of printing the word PASS if the
mark is larger than 50, printing the word FAIL if the
mark is larger than 30, and BAD FAIL if the mark is not
larger than 30.

(a)   4.1   IF mark larger than 50
       4.2   THEN
       4.3   PRINT "PASS"
       4.4   ELSEIF mark larger than 30
       4.5   THEN
       4.6   PRINT "FAIL"
       4.7   ELSE
       4.8   PRINT "BAD FAIL"
       4.9   ENDIF

(b)

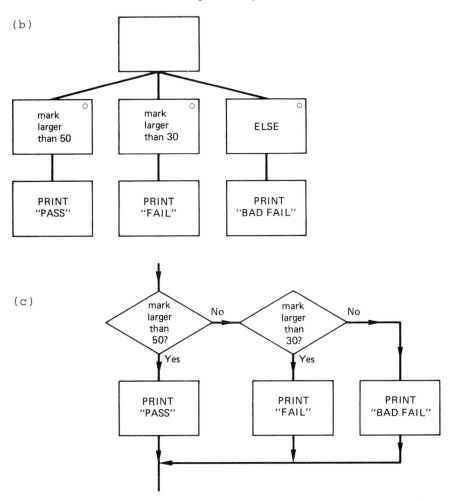

(c)

Figure 3.4

Note that type 3 can be extended to choose from any number of alternatives, but care must be taken in the wording of the condition and the order in which the alternatives are laid down. For example, above 4.4 has an implicit (and mark is not larger than 50) condition. The last "leg", that is ELSE (4.7 and 4.8 in figure 3.4a), need not be specified if there is no processing to be done. There is no restriction on the conditions used at each point (other than those inherent in implementing in BBC BASIC) - they can be testing different stores. However, the example above is the more common use.

In any of these first three types the conditions can be
as complex as required, the actual words used will be
discussed under the IF statement in chapter 4. For
example if we want to test month and day at the same
time we can use the process shown in figure 3.5.

(a)   5.1   IF month = 11 AND day = 5
       5.2   THEN
       5.3   PRINT "BONFIRE NIGHT"
       5.4   ENDIF

(b)

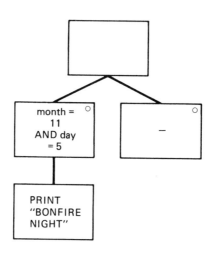

(c)

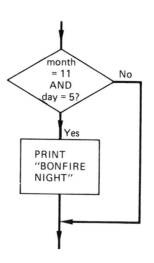

Figure 3.5

Type 4

This fourth type is very similar to type 3. However on many machines it is implemented differently from type 3 so it is useful to distinguish them at the design stage. We want to carry out a particular process according to the value in a store or as the result of a calculation. Hence, if the value is 1 we want to carry out a first process, if it is 2 a second process, if it is 3 a third process and so on (that is, we are choosing 1 from many). We should also cater for the default case where the value is none of those specified. This construct caters only for integer values starting at 1. In any event we would then proceed to the next process in the sequence.

In the example of figure 3.6 we wish to carry out process A if recordtype is 1 or 4, process B if recordtype is 2, process C if recordtype is 3 and process D otherwise. Note that we can test only one store or check the same calculation in each case.

(a)   6.1   CASE recordtype is 1 or 4
       6.2   process A
       6.3   CASE recordtype is 2
       6.4   process B
       6.5   CASE recordtype is 3
       6.6   process C
       6.7   CASE default
       6.8   process D
       6.9   ENDCASE

(b)

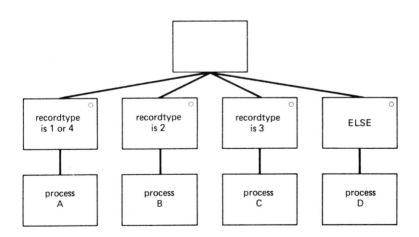

(c)

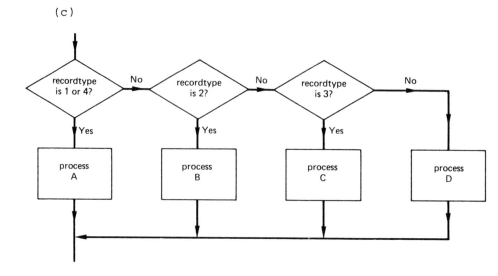

Figure 3.6

3.4 Iteration

An iteration consists of repeating a process either an integral number of times or while some condition is true. There are other forms of iteration but I have found these two to be sufficient. (Most designers include at least a third type of iteration - repeat until a condition is true - but I do not find it necessary for use in design and it is more straightforward, particularly for beginners, if there are only two types to consider.)

Iteration is really only a fancy word for loop, so the process to be repeated is enclosed inside the words LOOP and ENDLOOP.

Type 1

In this first type we want to carry out a particular process an integral number of times, the exact number being determined by the values specified for start, end and gap (see figure 3.7). For instance, if we specify start as 2, end as 8 and gap as 3, we are stating that we want the process carried out for kount = 2, 5 and 8 (that is, in this example we will print the three numbers 2, 5 and 8). This design construct includes the zero case (where we do not want the process in the loop carried out at all); for example, start is 8, end is 2 and gap is 3.

(a)   7.1 LOOP kount from start to end by gap
        7.2   PRINT kount
        7.3 ENDLOOP

(b)

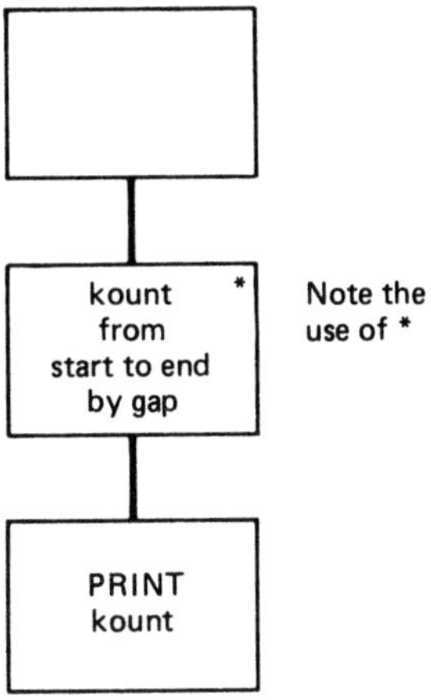

```
            kount      *     Note the
            from             use of *
         start to end
            by gap


            PRINT
            kount
```

(c)

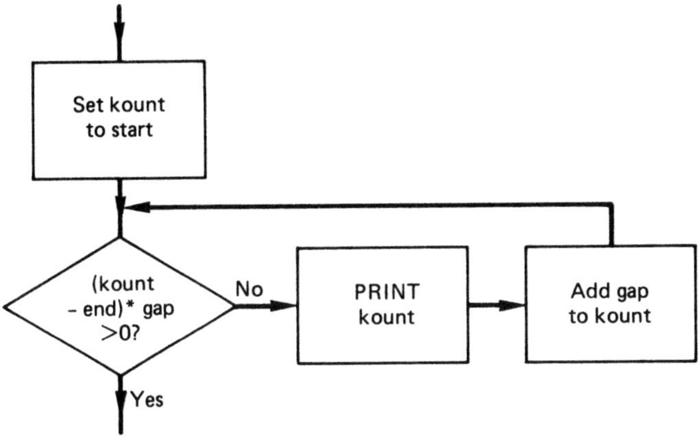

Figure 3.7

Type 2

In this second type we want to carry out a particular
process while a condidion is true. We must ensure that
the condition can be tested properly; often we need to
initialise a store or obtain some data (see figure 3.9)
before entering the loop. This design construct
includes the zero case (that is, where we do not want
the process in the loop carried out at all because the
condition is false when we attempt to enter the loop
the first time).

(a)   8.1 LOOP while sum < 1000
        8.2   PRINT number
        8.3   sum = sum + number
        8.4   INPUT number
        8.5 ENDLOOP

(b)

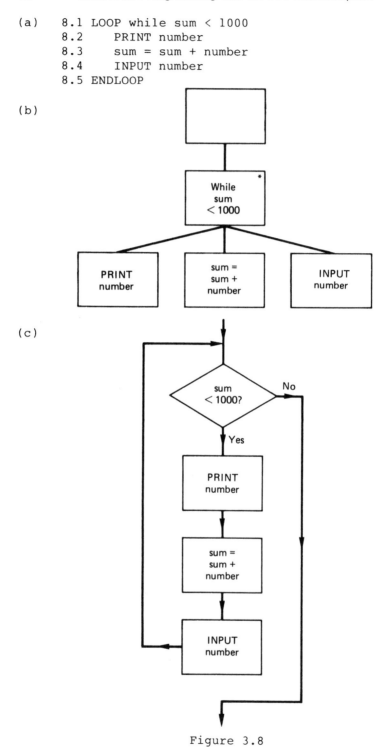

(c)

Figure 3.8

The example shown in figure 3.9 illustrates the initialisation necessary (7.1) for the loop condition to be correctly checked. Note also the READ-AHEAD (7.2) to simplify the processing required in the loop. The READ at 8.4 is sometimes called the READ-TO-REPLACE and can provide the READ-AHEAD for the next while loop if desired.

(a)   7.1 sum = zero
       7.2 INPUT number
       8.1 LOOP while sum < 1000
       8.2   PRINT number
       8.3   sum = sum + number
       8.4   INPUT number
       8.5 ENDLOOP

(b)

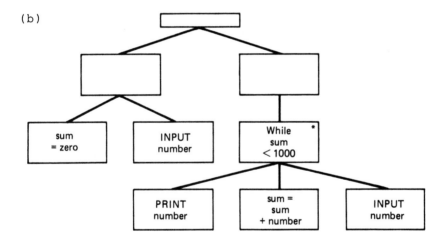

(c)

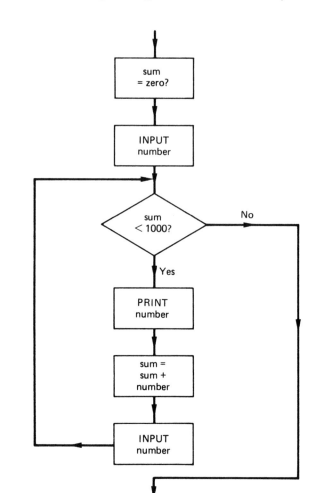

Figure 3.9

3.5 Nesting

Nesting is merely the method whereby a complete program is described; that is, we embed sequences inside selections, iterations inside sequences etc. - whatever we need to solve our problem.

Figure 3.10 shows an example of a sequence (9.3) inside a selection (9).

(a)   9.1   IF mark larger than 50
        9.2   THEN
        9.31   PRINT "PASS"
        9.32   p=p+1
        9.4   ENDIF

(b)

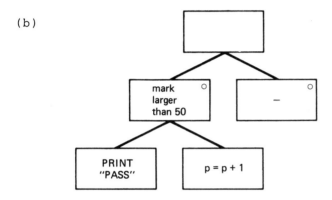

(c)

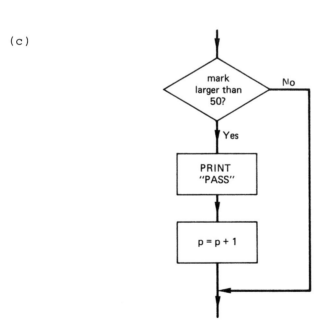

Figure 3.10

Figure 3.11 is an example of two sequences (10.3 and 10.5) nested in the true and false legs of a selection (10).

(a)   10.1   IF mark larger than 50
        10.2   THEN
        10.31   PRINT "PASS"
        10.32   p=p+1
        10.4   ELSE
        10.51   PRINT "FAIL"
        10.52   f=f+1
        10.6   ENDIF

(b)

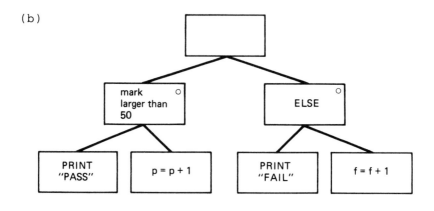

(c)

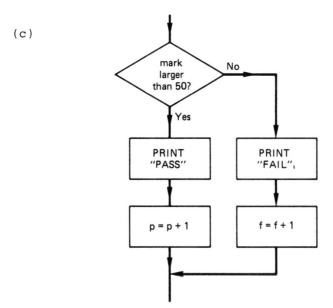

Figure 3.11

Figure 3.12 is an example of three sequences (11.3, 11.6 and 11.8) nested in each of the legs of a selection (11).

(a)   11.1   IF mark larger than 50
          11.2   THEN
          11.31   PRINT "PASS"
          11.32   p=p+1
          11.4   ELSEIF mark larger than 30
          11.5   THEN
          11.61   PRINT "FAIL"
          11.62   f=f+1
          11.7   ELSE
          11.81   PRINT "BAD FAIL"
          11.82   b=b+1
          11.9   ENDIF

(b)

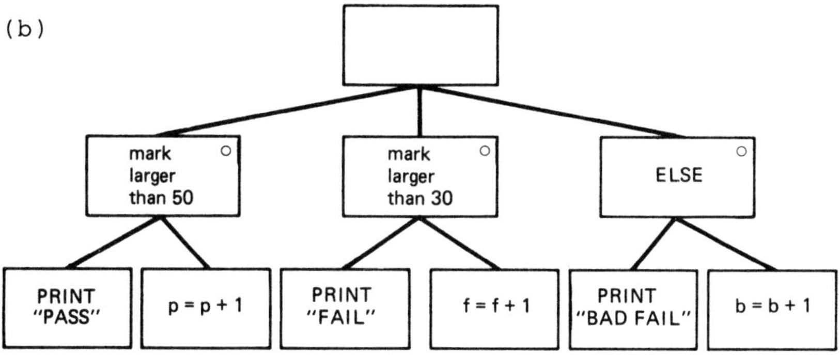

(c)

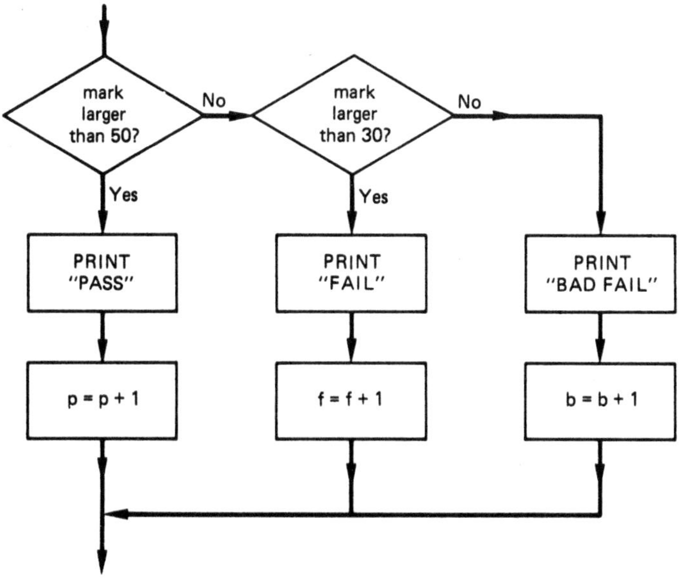

Figure 3.12

Figure 3.13 shows a Type 1 selection (12.3) nested in the true leg of a Type 1 selection (12).

(a)   12.1   IF month = 11
       12.2   THEN
       12.31   IF day = 5
       12.32   THEN
       12.331   PRINT "BONFIRE NIGHT"
       12.34   ENDIF
       12.4   ENDIF

(b)

(c)

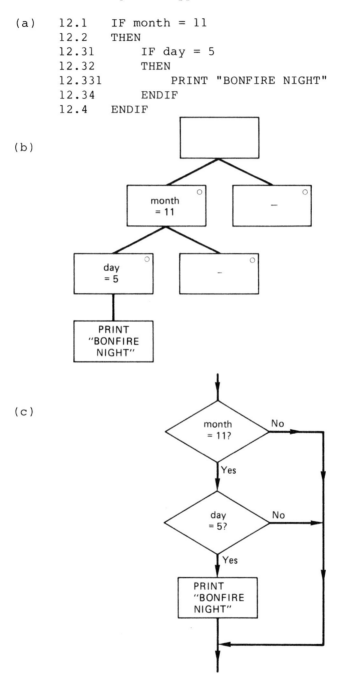

Figure 3.13

Figure 3.14 is an example of a Type 2 selection (13.3) nested in the true leg of a Type 2 selection (13).

(a) 13.1   IF month = 11
     13.2   THEN
     13.31   IF day = 5
     13.32   THEN
     13.331   PRINT "BONFIRE NIGHT"
     13.34   ELSE
     13.351   PRINT "WRONG DAY"
     13.36   ENDIF
     13.4   ELSE
     13.5   PRINT "WRONG MONTH"
     13.6   ENDIF

(b)

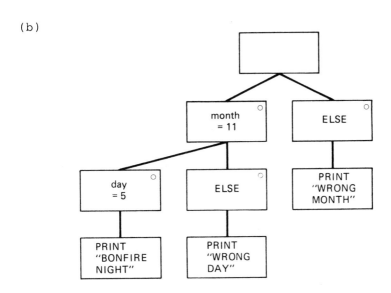

(c)

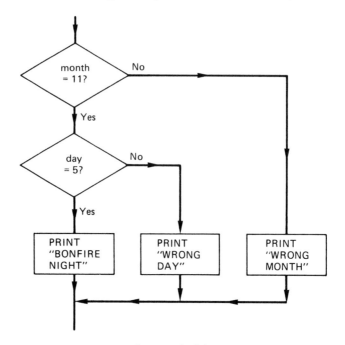

Figure 3.14

Figure 3.15 shows an example of a sequence (14.2) nested in an iteration (14).

(a)   14.1 LOOP kount from start to end by gap
        14.21   PRINT kount
        14.22   sum=sum+kount
        14.3 ENDLOOP

(b)

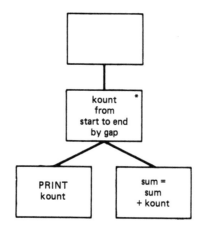

(c)

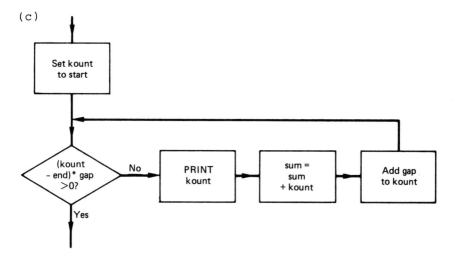

Figure 3.15

Figure 3.16 is an example of an iteration (15.2) nested in an iteration (15).

(a) 15.1 LOOP kount from start to end by gap
     15.21   LOOP number from 7 to 3 by -1
     15.221   PRINT kount * number
     15.23   ENDLOOP
     15.3 ENDLOOP

(b)

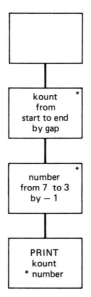

(c)

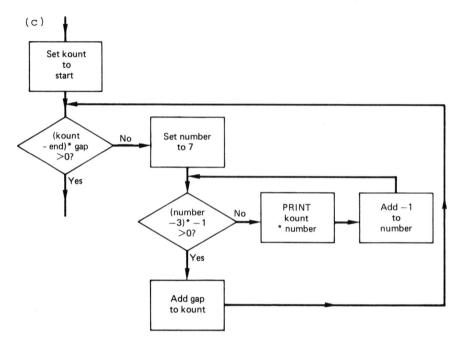

Figure 3.16

Finally, figure 3.17 is an example of a sequence (16.2) nested in an iteration (16). Note, however, that this is an incorrect design! Since sum never changes, if we enter the loop we will never get out again!

(a)   16.1 LOOP while sum < 1000
        16.21   PRINT number
        16.22   INPUT number
        16.4 ENDLOOP

(b)

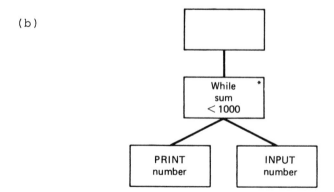

(c)

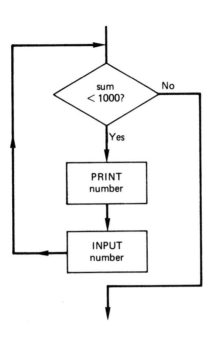

Figure 3.17

3.6 Modules

If we design a program using top-down we have split the program up logically and, if we wish to, we can use the two modular techniques of subroutines and procedures to implement a whole or part sequence, a selection or an iteration. It means also that if there is some part of the program that is going to give more difficulty than the other parts, then we can isolate it as part of a sequence and formally design and code it later. If the program being designed is intended for more than one make of micro, it is also a good idea to try to isolate the machine-dependent features into separate modules at the design stage. In addition, if it is known that particular sections are likely to be too slow or too big, try to design these into separate modules for easy translation into assembly language if necessary.

3.7 Small Example Program

In order to illustrate the top-down technique described above, consider the following small example program.

It is required to produce a program to check the capital city of three countries as "guessed" by a student at a terminal and to reply "CORRECT" or give the correct answer as appropriate. We will call this

Version 1 of the specification. The number of countries is restricted to three to keep the program data small; it could be any number. A suggested design is shown in figure 3.18.

```
1.   Print heading
2.   Ask 3 questions
3.   Finish
```

Break down step 2

```
2.1  LOOP count from 1 to 3
2.2     Ask a question
2.3  ENDLOOP
```

Break down step 2.2

```
2.21  Get question and answer from data
2.22  Print question
2.23  Get reply
2.24   IF reply = answer
2.25   THEN
2.26       print "CORRECT"
2.27   ELSE
2.28       print answer
2.29   ENDIF
```

Therefore the complete design is

```
1.   Print heading
2.1  LOOP count from 1 to 3
2.21   Get question and answer from data
2.22   Print question
2.23   Get reply
2.24    IF reply = answer
2.25    THEN
2.26        print "CORRECT"
2.27    ELSE
2.28        print answer
2.29    ENDIF
2.3  ENDLOOP
3.   Finish
```

Figure 3.18

If you prefer the diagrammatic version, it will look like figure 3.19.

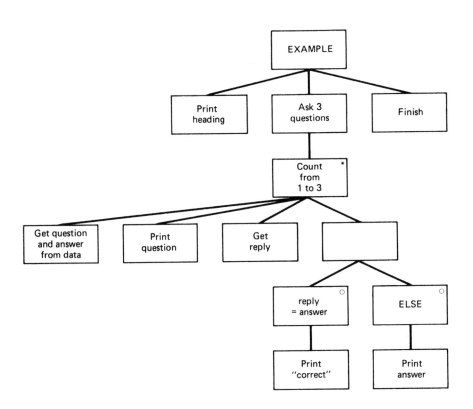

Figure 3.19

The flowchart version is also included (figure 3.20) for completeness.

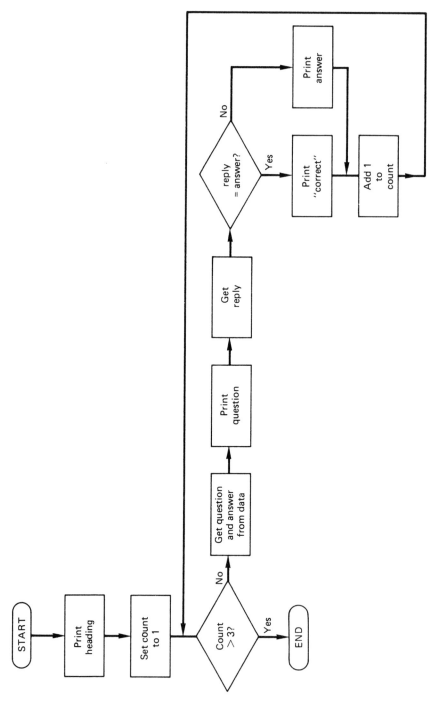

Figure 3.20

The user, however, is not quite satisfied with
this. He would like to know how many answers were
correct. This is Version 2 of the specification!
The additional operations are

(a) to initialise the number of correct answers to zero
(b) to add 1 to the number of correct answers each time
    that a reply is found to correct
(c) to print out the number of correct answers.

Using the top-down method it should be easy to spot
that

(i)   (a) must be done before the loop
(ii) (b) must be done within the loop and also within
      the correct path of the selection
(iii) (c) must be done after the loop.

Version 1 of the design can therefore be amended to
produce Version 2 by incorporating the changes
specified as shown in figure 3.21.
The diagrammatic version is shown in figure 3.22.

```
1.1    Print heading
1.2    Initialise correct to zero
2.1    LOOP count from 1 to 3
2.21      Get question and answer from data
2.22      Print question
2.23      Get reply
2.24      IF reply = answer
2.25      THEN
2.261             print "CORRECT"
2.262             add 1 to correct
2.27      ELSE
2.28              print answer
2.29      ENDIF
3.3    ENDLOOP
3.1    Print number of correct answers
3.2    Finish
```

Figure 3.21

The flowchart is shown in figure 3.23.

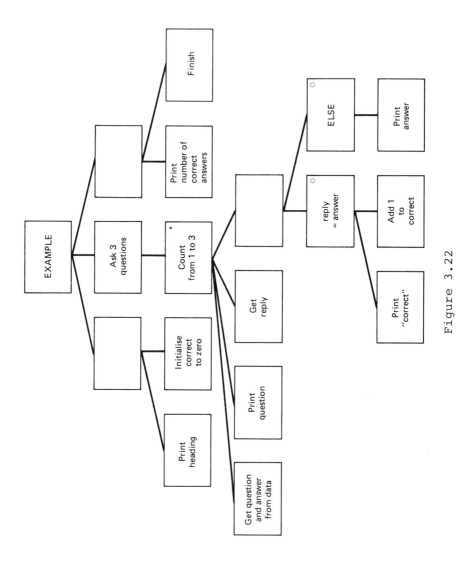

Figure 3.22

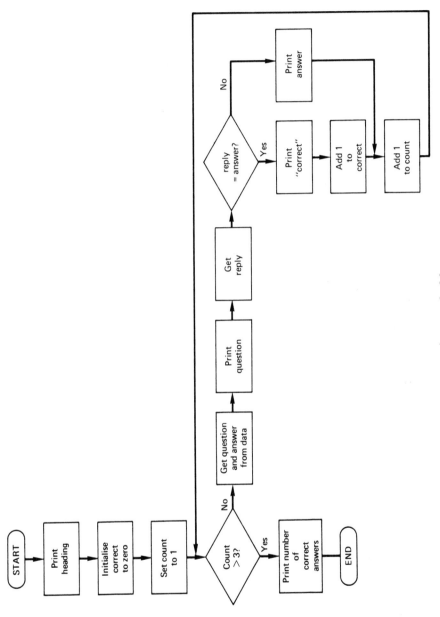

Figure 3.23

Note how much easier it is to work out the necessary operations and find their correct place when the first two representations of design are used rather than the flowchart.

The corresponding code is shown below. Note that FOR and NEXT will be found in chapter 5, and IF in chapter 4. You will find that this coding becomes clearer after you have read these two chapters.

A more comprehensive program design example with its coding will be found in chapter 6.

Coding (Version 1)

```
1000 PRINT "I WILL ASK YOU 3 GEOGRAPHY QUESTIONS"
2100 FOR count% = 1 TO 3
2210     READ ques$,ans$
2220     PRINT "WHAT IS THE CAPITAL OF ";ques$
2230     INPUT try$
2240     IF ans$=try$ THEN PRINT "CORRECT"
                     ELSE PRINT ans$

2300 NEXT count%
3000 END
8000 DATA "FRANCE"
8100 DATA "PARIS"
8200 DATA "ITALY"
8300 DATA "ROME"
8400 DATA "JAPAN"
8500 DATA "TOKYO"
```

Coding (Version 2)

```
1100 PRINT "I WILL ASK YOU 3 GEOGRAPHY QUESTIONS"
1200 correct%=0
2100 FOR count% = 1 TO 3
2210     READ ques$,ans$
2220     PRINT "WHAT IS THE CAPITAL OF      ";ques$
2230     INPUT try$
2240     IF ans$=try$ THEN PRINT
     "CORRECT":correct%=correct%+1
                     ELSE PRINT ans$

2300 NEXT count%
3100 PRINT "NUMBER CORRECT =   ";correct%
3200 END
8000 DATA "FRANCE"
8100 DATA "PARIS"
8200 DATA "ITALY"
8300 DATA "ROME"
8400 DATA "JAPAN"
8500 DATA "TOKYO"
```

3.8 Summary

The top-down method described enables a complex problem to be broken down into simpler logical parts without worrying about the intricacies of the coding. It is necessary, however, to know the elementary actions that can be carried out.

Using the method it is possible to produce good, well-structured programs for the BBC micro, and also to provide a design that could easily be implemented on other machines.

A complete program design example will be found in chapter 6.

4 Coding Decisions in BASIC

4.1 Introduction
At various points in our program we will want to make decisions, and in BASIC there are two statements available to do this

    the IF statement

and

    the ON statement.

We will discuss these statements and then select how best to use them.

4.2 The IF Statement
The IF statement requires a condition to be tested. BASIC has six conditions, each represented by its own symbol as listed below

Condition	Symbol
is equal to	=
is not equal to	<>
is less than	<
is greater than	>
is less than or equal to	<=
is greater than or equal to	>=

Thus

    IF number < 16 ...

is interpreted as, IF number is less than 16..., and "number < 16 " is referred to as the "condition".
   The result of the condition test is either TRUE or FALSE. The test can be numeric, as above, or alphanumeric. For example

    IF name$ = "SMITH" ...

    IF name1$ > name2$ ...

There is also a boolean test: zero is treated as FALSE and therefore all other values are TRUE. For example

        IF contents ...

is equivalent to

        IF contents <> 0 ...

In this context, using the numeric rather than the boolean test is probably easier to understand, but further uses of the boolean test will be given later.

Where it is necessary to test more than one condition (known as a compound condition), we can use the logical operators AND and OR as applicable. An example with AND is

IF day$ = "MONDAY" AND week = 1 ...

The result of this condition test is TRUE only if both the day is Monday and the week is 1. An example with OR is

IF day$ = "MONDAY" OR day$ = "TUESDAY" ...

The result of this condition test is TRUE if the day is either Monday or Tuesday.

AND and OR can be used together in the compound condition but brackets must be used to show the meaning and priority clearly. For example

IF (height > 7 AND sex$ ="M")
OR (height > 6 AND sex$ ="F")...

The result of this condition test is TRUE if either (a) height is greater than 7 and sex is M or (b) height is greater than 6 and sex is F.

There is another logical operator EOR which is less commonly used:

IF day$ ="SUNDAY" EOR time <= 7 ...

The result of this condition test will be TRUE if only one of the two individual conditions is true; that is, either (a) the day is Sunday but time is greater than 7 or (b) the day is not Sunday but time is less than or equal to 7. The result of the condition test is therefore FALSE if both of the individual conditions are true or if both are false.

There are two forms of the IF statement that I shall discuss.

IF condition THEN statement

and

IF condition THEN statement1 ELSE statement2

There is a third form (IF condition THEN linenumber) which I never use and do not like. It will therefore be ignored in this book.

The IF condition THEN statement is used when we wish to carry out some action if the result of the condition test is TRUE but to do nothing if it is false (except to continue with the next logical instruction).

The IF condition THEN statement1 ELSE statement2 is used when we wish to carry out a particular action if the result of the condition test is TRUE but to carry out an alternative action if it is FALSE.

Examples of the above two forms, expressed in ordinary English are

If it is raining then I will take my umbrella.
If it is snowing then I will wear my boots else I will wear my shoes.

4.3 The IF Condition THEN Statement

We have seen, in design, that decisions of this nature are described as in figure 4.1.

(a)   7.0 IF mark larger than 50
        7.1 THEN
        7.2   PRINT "PASS"
        7.3 ENDIF

(b)

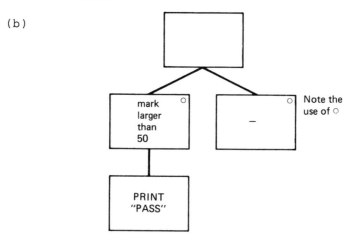

(c)

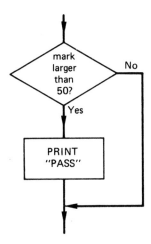

Figure 4.1

When we code this in BASIC we can write

70 IF mark > 50 THEN PRINT "PASS"

That is, we put the action required after the word
THEN.

    In most cases the word THEN can be omitted, but
personally I always include it to maintain readability.

    If we wish to carry out more than one action we can
put the instructions one after the other, separated by
a colon (:) up to the maximum line length (230). For
example

80 IF mark > 50 THEN PRINT "PASS" : p = p + 1
90 IF aliens% = 0 THEN PRINT "YOU WIN" : END

These lines are called multistatement lines and will
often exceed a single line on the screen. When entering
the program from the keyboard, you must be careful not
to press the RETURN key until you have typed in the
whole line.

    There are two problems with IF... THEN... which may
well already be apparent. Firstly, what happens when
the IF... THEN... needed exceeds the maximum line
length? Secondly, is it not possible to preserve the
indentation used in design?

    We will return to these two problems after the
explanation of the IF... THEN... ELSE... .

4.4 The IF Condition THEN Statement1 ELSE Statement2

We have seen, in design, that decisions of this nature are described as in figure 4.2.

(a)   7.0 IF mark larger than 50
       7.1 THEN
       7.2   PRINT "PASS"
       7.3 ELSE
       7.4   PRINT "FAIL"
       7.5 ENDIF

(b)

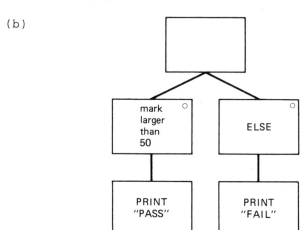

(c)

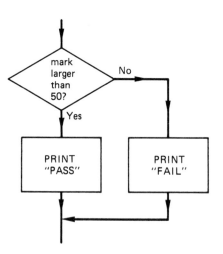

Figure 4.2

When we code this in BASIC we can write

70 IF mark > 50 THEN PRINT "PASS" ELSE PRINT "FAIL"

That is, we put the actions for the conditon test is
TRUE after THEN, and the alternative actions after
ELSE.
    We can again use the multistatement line. For
example

70 IF mark > 50 THEN PRINT "PASS" : p = p + 1 ELSE
PRINT "FAIL" : f = f + 1

The two problems of maximum line length and loss of
indentation are again with us.

4.5 Use of GOTO to Overcome the Limit on Line Length and to Preserve Indentation

The GOTO is a dangerous instruction since it allows
control within a program to be transferred directly to
any line number. However, if used in a proper and
consistent manner it can be helpful in solving the two
problems referred to above. Another solution uses
procedures or subroutines (see chapter 7).
    We shall look at IF... THEN... ELSE... first, and
then IF... THEN... .
    The layout for IF... THEN... ELSE... will be more
like top-down if we code using GOTO after THEN and
ELSE. For example, the design

```
2.1   IF mark larger than 50
2.105 THEN
2.11      PRINT "PASS"
2.12      p=p+1
2.2   ELSE
2.21      PRINT "FAIL"
2.22      f=f+1
2.9   ENDIF
```

would be coded as

```
2100 IF mark > 50 THEN GOTO 2110 ELSE GOTO 2200
2110     PRINT "PASS"
2120     p = p + 1
2199     GOTO 2999
2200 REM DEFAULT
2210     PRINT "FAIL"
2220     f = f + 1
2999 REM ENDIF 2100
```

Indentation is thus preserved and multistatement lines
are avoided. The maximum line length can still be
exceeded by a very long condition!
    As a second example, the design

```
2.1    IF mark larger than 50
2.105 THEN
2.11       PRINT "PASS"
2.12       p=p+1
2.2    ELSEIF mark  larger than 30
2.205 THEN
2.21       PRINT "FAIL"
2.22       f=f+1
2.3    ELSE
2.31       PRINT "BAD FAIL"
2.32       b=b+1
2.9    ENDIF
```

would be coded as

```
2100 IF mark > 50 THEN GOTO 2110 ELSE GOTO 2200
2110     PRINT "PASS"
2120     p = p + 1
2199     GOTO 2999
2200 IF mark > 30 THEN GOTO 2210 ELSE GOTO 2300
2210     PRINT "FAIL"
2220     f = f + 1
2299     GOTO 2999
2300 REM DEFAULT
2310     PRINT "BAD FAIL"
2320     b = b + 1
2999 REM ENDIF 2100
```

    The layout for IF... THEN... will also be more like
top-down if we code using GOTO after THEN and ELSE. For
example

```
2.1    IF mark larger than 50
2.105 THEN
2.11       PRINT "PASS"
2.12       p=p+1
2.9    ENDIF
```

would be coded as

```
2100 IF mark > 50 THEN GOTO 2110 ELSE GOTO 2200
2110     PRINT "PASS"
2120     p = p + 1
2199     GOTO 2999
2200 REM DEFAULT
2999 REM ENDIF 2100
```

Indentation is also preserved here and again multistatement lines are avoided. The maximum line length can also be exceeded here by a very long condition! We could also code a shorter version using a different condition. For example

```
2100 IF mark <=50 THEN GOTO 2200
2110    PRINT "PASS"
2120    p = p + 1
2200 REM ENDIF 2100
```

However, we have had to reverse the original condition, which is a potential source of error.

Conditions	Reversed conditions
=	<>
<>	=
<	>=
>	<=
<=	>
>=	<

There is less likelihood of error if we code using NOT. For instance

```
2100 IF NOT ( mark > 50 ) THEN GOTO 2200
```

We must enclose the condition in brackets - without the brackets this instruction is accepted as a boolean test, with different results. For a compound condition, therefore, we must enclose the whole of the condition in the brackets. For example

```
80 IF NOT ( age < 25 AND sex$="M" ) THEN PRINT
   "INELIGIBLE"
```

4.6 THEN IF and ELSE IF
It is possible to use IF immediately after THEN and also after ELSE. Extreme care should be exercised when this is done.
    Consider the following structure:

```
    IF month = 11
    THEN
        IF day = 5
        THEN
            PRINT "BONFIRE NIGHT"
        ENDIF
    ENDIF
```

This could be coded as

```
100 IF month = 11 THEN IF day = 5 THEN PRINT "BONFIRE
    NIGHT"
```

which will work successfully.
    Personally I prefer to use the structure

```
    IF month = 11 AND day = 5
    THEN
        PRINT "BONFIRE NIGHT"
    ENDIF
```

coded as

```
100 IF month = 11 AND day = 5 THEN PRINT "BONFIRE
    NIGHT"
```

which will also work successfully.
    But now consider the structure

```
    IF month = 11
    THEN
        IF day = 5
        THEN
            PRINT "BONFIRE NIGHT"
        ELSE
            PRINT "WRONG DAY"
        ENDIF
    ELSE
        PRINT "WRONG MONTH"
    ENDIF
```

We might be tempted to code this as

```
100 IF month = 11 THEN IF day = 5 THEN PRINT "BONFIRE
    NIGHT" ELSE PRINT "WRONG DAY" ELSE PRINT "WRONG
    MONTH"
```

This instruction will be accepted and will print
"BONFIRE NIGHT" if both conditions are true but will
print "WRONG DAY" if either (or both) of the conditions
is (are) false.
    There is no problem if we use GOTO as shown
previously. The code for the above design is then

```
21000 IF month =11 THEN GOTO 21100
        ELSE GOTO 22000
21100 IF day = 5 THEN GOTO 21110
        ELSE GOTO 21200
21110        PRINT "BONFIRE NIGHT"
```

```
21199          GOTO 21999
21200 REM DEFAULT
21210          PRINT "WRONG DAY"
21999          GOTO 29999 : REM ENDIF 21100
22000 REM DEFAULT
22100     PRINT "WRONG MONTH"
29999 REM ENDIF 21000
```

Note that we have here a method to resolve the problem of a complicated condition that exceeds the maximum line length: that is, we merely split the original condition into several smaller conditions. For example, the structure

```
IF (year% MOD 4 = 0) AND ( NOT (year% MOD 100 = 0)
OR (year% MOD 400 = 0))
THEN
     PRINT "LEAP YEAR"
```

can be converted to

```
IF year% MOD 4 = 0
THEN IF NOT (year% MOD 100 = 0 )
     THEN
          PRINT "LEAP YEAR"
     ELSE IF year% MOD 400 = 0
          THEN
               PRINT "LEAP YEAR"
          ENDIF
     ENDIF
ENDIF
```

and coded by following the same rules as above. That is

```
10000 IF year% MOD 4 = 0 THEN GOTO 11000 ELSE GOTO
      12000
11000 IF NOT ( year% MOD 100 = 0 ) THEN GOTO 11100 ELSE

      GOTO 11200
11100          PRINT "LEAP YEAR"
11199          GOTO 11999
11200 IF year% MOD 400 = 0 THEN GOTO  11210 ELSE GOTO
      11220
11210               PRINT "LEAP YEAR"
11219               GOTO 11299
11220 REM DEFAULT
11299 REM ENDIF 11200
11999 REM ENDIF 11000
12000 REM DEFAULT
19999 REM ENDIF 10000
```

4.7 Summary of IF

The IF statement is powerful in BASIC but, because there is no inherent block structure and because of the maximum line length, it is essential to formulate particular ways (involving GOTO) of preserving structure, indentation and, in some cases, correct interpretation!

There is a preferred alternative approach - using procedures or subroutines that are available on the BBC micro - which will be discussed in chapter 7. However, procedures and/or subroutines are not available on all micros and thus some of the ideas above may need to be implemented.

4.8 The ON Statement

There are two general formats for this statement:

    ON expression GOTO... ELSE...

    ON expression GOSUB... ELSE...

Both formats allow a JUMP (danger!) to either (a) one of a number of lines (GOTO) or (b) one of a number of subroutines (GOSUB), depending on the value of the expression. For example

70 ON recordtype% GOTO 500,600,200,500

means jump to line number 500 if recordtype is 1 or 4, to 600 if recordtype is 2, or to 200 if recordtype is 3. It represents the design shown in figure 4.3.

```
(a)    CASE recordtype is 1 or 4
            process A
       CASE recordtype is 2
            process B
       CASE recordtype is 3
            process C
       ENDCASE
```

(b)

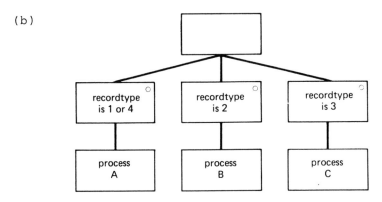

(c)

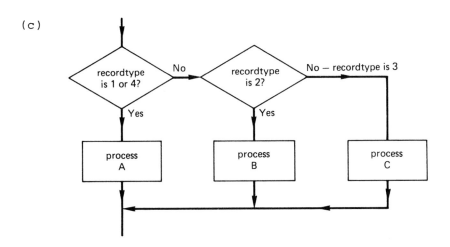

Figure 4.3

Here process A is coded at line 500, process B at line
600 and process C at line 200.
    But what happens if recordtype is not 1, 2, 3 or 4?
In that case an error will be indicated when the
program is run. It is far easier and safer to
incorporate the ELSE to specify what is to happen if
recordtype is not within the correct range. For
example, the simple insertion of the ELSE clause

70 ON recordtype% GOTO 500,600,200,500
   ELSE PRINT "INVALID RECTYPE"

is better than taking no action if the recordtype is
outside the range. Note that only one statement is
allowed after ELSE. If you want more than one statement
you must use a subroutine or procedure (see chapter 7)
or use GOTO.

Good programs will always use ELSE, and also each of the actions carried out at the specified line numbers should return (by means of GOTO) to the next logical instruction. For example

```
2100 On recordtype% GOTO 2200,2300 ELSE PRINT"incorrect
     data - ignored"
2110 PRINT s
2120 END
2200      t1=t1 + 1
2210      s=s + t1
2220 GOTO 2110
2300      t2=t2 + 1
2310      s=s - t2
2320 GOTO 2110
```

Using GOSUB rather than GOTO is similar, and will be discussed in chapter 7.

4.9 Summary of ON
The ON statement is useful for coding CASE decisions. It will appear in good programs provided that the ELSE clause is always used and return is always made to the next logical instruction.

4.10 Summary
Provided that design has been carried out in sufficient detail, coding for decisions can become a purely mechanical process if some of the implementations suggested above are used in a consistent manner, or if procedures or subroutines (see chapter 7) are used.

5 Coding Loops in BASIC

5.1 Introduction
At various points in a program we will want to construct loops, and in BASIC there are two statements available for this:

the FOR statement

and

the REPEAT statement.

We will discuss these statements and then select how best to use them.

5.2 The FOR Statement
The FOR statement enables a sequence of instructions to be executed a number of times using a "COUNTER". The sequence of instructions is placed between the FOR statement and a NEXT statement. For example

```
1000 FOR ...
1100
1200
1300
1400 NEXT ...
```

We have seen, in design, that loops which are executed a specified number of times are needed. These are described as in figure 5.1.

```
(a)    7.1 LOOP kount from start to end by gap
       7.2     PRINT kount
       7.3        sum=sum+kount
       7.4 ENDLOOP
```

(b)

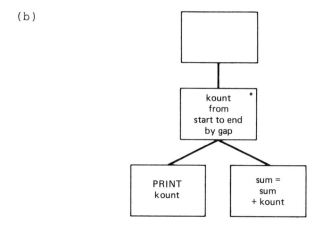

(c)

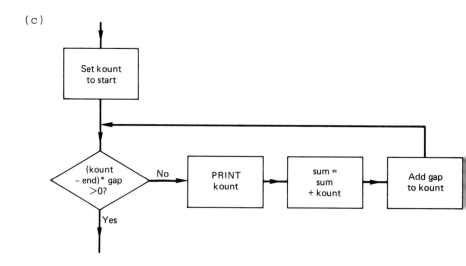

Figure 5.1

We need to examine the FOR ... NEXT statement in order to implement this design.

5.3 FOR ... NEXT (Integer Variables)

```
10 FOR number% = 1 TO 4
20    PRINT number%
30 NEXT number%
```

This code has set up a loop which is executed four times, the variable number% has the value 1 the first time, 2 the second time and so on. Therefore the output from this code is

      1
      2
      3
      4

The variable name after NEXT can be omitted (to make
the program faster), but personally I always include it
to maintain readability. In any case, it can always be
removed later if necessary.
   The actions that we wish to carry out are placed on
successive lines but, if the number of instructions is
small, we can put the instructions one after the other
separated by a colon (:) up to the maximum line length
(230). For example

```
10 FOR number% =1 TO 4
20     PRINT number%
30     PRINT number% * 2
40 NEXT number%
```

can be coded as

```
10 FOR number% = 1 TO 4 : PRINT number% : PRINT number%
* 2 : NEXT number%
```

These lines are called multistatement lines and will
often exceed a single line on the screen. When entering
the program from the keyboard, you must be careful not
to press the RETURN key until you have typed in the
whole line. Indentation is also lost.
   The output from this program is

      1
      2
      2
      4
      3
      6
      4
      8

The variable specified is automatically increased by
1 each time that we go round the loop. However, we can
specify the increment if a value other than 1 is
needed, or specify a decrement. An increment is
specified as in the following example.

```
40 FOR number% = 3 TO 7 STEP 2
50     PRINT number%
60 NEXT number%
```

This loop will output

```
    3
    5
    7
```

A decrement is specified as

```
240 FOR number% = 7 TO 3 STEP -1
250     PRINT number%
260 NEXT number%
```

This loop will output

```
    7
    6
    5
    4
    3
```

The starting value, finishing value and step value need not be constants; each of them can be a constant or a variable name, or an expression.For example

```
430 FOR kount% = start% TO end% STEP gap%
440     PRINT kount%
450 NEXT kount%
```

Assuming that start% contains 3, end% contains 7 and gap% contains 2, then the output from this loop will be

```
    3
    5
    7
```

Another example is

```
460 FOR kount% = p% - q% TO p% + q% STEP x% + y%
470     PRINT kount%
480 NEXT kount%
```

Assuming that p% contains 6, q% contains 4, x% contains 1 and y% contains 0, then the output from this loop will be

```
    2
    3
    4
    5
    6
```

```
 7
 8
 9
10
```

The FOR ... NEXT statement is often used to code a loop where we are required to refer to elements in an array. Note the use of the "counter" as the subscript for the array.

The next two examples show data being entered to fill an array. The first case uses data from the keyboard (INPUT).

```
10 DIM arrayname$(10)
20 FOR row% = 1 TO 10
30   INPUT "PLEASE ENTER NEXT NAME",arrayname$(row%)
40 NEXT row%
50 END
```

while the second uses data contained in the program (READ)

```
 10 DIM nos%(8)
 20 FOR count% = 1 TO 8
 30      READ nos%(count%)
 40 NEXT count%
 50 END
100 DATA 3,7,54,0,8,6,4,8
```

So far we have considered only integer variables for controlling loops, but we may wish to use real variables. However, where integer values are sufficient, integer variables should be used to control the loop as this can speed up operation by a factor of 3 compared to the use of real variables.

5.4 FOR ... NEXT (Real Variables)
We must ensure that a real variable is specified when we wish the "COUNTER" to take real values. For example

```
70 FOR number = 1.1 TO 4.1
80    PRINT number
90 NEXT number
```

This code has set up a loop which is executed four times. The variable number has the value 1.1 the first time, 2.1 the second time and so on. Therefore the

64 Good BASIC Programming with the BBC Microcomputer

output from this code is

```
1.1
2.1
3.1
4.1
```

The variable name after NEXT can be omitted (to make the program faster) but personally I always include it to maintain readability. Note that it can always be removed later if necessary.

The actions that we wish to carry out are placed on successive lines but, if the number of instructions is small, we can put the instructions one after the other separated by a colon (:) up to the maximum line length (230). For example

```
10 FOR number =1.1 TO 4.1
20    PRINT number
30    PRINT number * 2
40 NEXT number
```

can be coded as

```
10 FOR number = 1.1 TO  4.1  :  PRINT  number  :  PRINT
number * 2 : NEXT number
```

These lines are also multistatement lines and will thus often exceed a single line on the screen. Once again, when entering the program from the keyboard you must be careful not to press the RETURN key until you have typed in the whole line. Indentation is also lost.

The output from this program is

```
1.1
2.2
2.1
4.2
3.1
6.2
4.1
8.2
```

The variable specified is automatically increased by 1 each time that we go round the loop, but we can specify an increment other than 1 as in the following example.

```
100 FOR number = 3.3 TO 7.5 STEP .3
110    PRINT number
120 NEXT number
```

This loop will output
    3.3
    3.6
    3.9
    4.2
    4.5
    4.8
    5.1
    5.4
    5.7
    6
    6.3
    6.60000001
    6.90000001
    7.20000001

This example has highlighted the problem of accuracy in loops controlled by real variables. This loop is executed 14 times, not 15 as you might expect, because the control variable has now reached the value 7.50000001 and the loop is therefore inactive.
    A decrement can be expressed as in the next example.

```
300 FOR number = 7.5 TO 3.3 STEP -.3
310     PRINT number
320 NEXT number
```

The output from this loop is
    7.5
    7.2
    6.9
    6.6
    6.3
    6
    5.7
    5.39999999
    5.09999999
    4.79999999
    4.49999999
    4.19999999
    3.89999999
    3.59999999

Again the same problem of inaccuracy occurs.
    The starting value, finishing value and step value need not be constants; each of them can be a constant or a variable name, or an expression. For example

```
430 FOR kount = start TO end STEP gap
440     PRINT kount
450 NEXT kount
```

Assuming that start contains 3.1, end contains 7.1 and gap contains 2.3, then the output from this loop will be

        3.1
        5.4

It should now be apparent that we can code the initial design in figure 5.1 as

```
710 FOR kount = start TO end STEP gap
720     PRINT kount
730     sum=sum + kount
740 NEXT kount
```

5.5 Nested Loops
We have seen, in design, that loops of this nature are described as in figure 5.2.

(a)   7.1 LOOP kount from start to end by gap
       7.2   LOOP number from 7 to 3 by -1
       7.3   PRINT kount * number
       7.4   ENDLOOP
       7.5 ENDLOOP

(b)

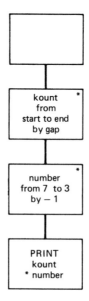

(c)

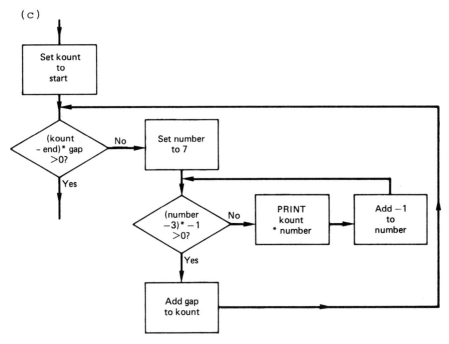

Figure 5.2

When we code this in BASIC we can write

```
500 FOR kount% = start% TO end% STEP gap%
510    FOR number% = 7 TO 3 STEP -1
520        PRINT kount% * number%
530    NEXT number%
540 NEXT kount%
```

Assuming that start% contains 3, end% contains 7 and gap% contains 2, the output will be

```
       21
       18
       15
       12
        9
       35
       30
       25
       20
       15
       49
       42
       35
       28
       21
```

That is, for each time round the outer loop all the values in the inner loop are processed.

If the variable names are omitted from the NEXT statement, the results are the same, but I believe that the code is then less easy to understand. For example

```
600 FOR kount% = start% TO end% STEP gap%
610    FOR number% = 7 TO 3 STEP -1
620        PRINT kount% * number%
630    NEXT
640 NEXT
```

You must be careful not to re-use a variable that is still in use. For example

```
810 FOR kount% = start% TO end% STEP gap%
820    FOR kount% = 7 TO 3 STEP -1
830        PRINT kount%
840    NEXT
850 NEXT
```

This code will be accepted, but it will have unpredictable results depending on the contents of start%, end% and gap%. For example, with start%=3, end%=7 and gap%=2, an infinite loop has been constructed: the outer loop will never be exhausted and the numbers printed in the inner loop are continuously output.

Nested FOR loops are often used to manipulate data in two-dimensional arrays. In the following example, data is transferred from the DATA statements into a 5 by 20 array, one column at a time. That is, the numbers 1 to 20 from line 100 are transferred into table(1,1) , table(1,2), table(1,3), ... table(1,20) respectively , then the numbers from line 200 are transferred into table(2,1), table(2,2), table(2,3) ... table(2,20) respectively, then the numbers from line 300 are transferred into table(3,1) to table(3,20), from line 400 into table(4,1) to table(4,20), and from line 500 into table(5,1) to table(5,20). Twenty data items have been grouped on each data line. This is merely for convenience and clarity. Any number of data lines can be used.

```
10 DIM table(5,20)
20 FOR row% = 1 TO 5
25    FOR col% = 1 TO 20
30        READ table(row%,col%)
35    NEXT col%
40 NEXT row%
50 END
```

```
100 DATA 1,2,3,4,5,6,7,8,9,10,11,12,13,14,15,16,17,18,
    19,20
200 DATA -1,-2,-3,-4,-5,-6,0,0,0,0,0,0,0,0,0,0,0,0,0,0
300 DATA 1,2,3,2,4,9,7,6,5,4,8,9,9,0,1,2,3,4,5,6
400 DATA 1,6,9,8,4,76,5,7,6,4,6,5,0,5,8,76,4,3,7,45
500 DATA 4,9,9,9,0,7,0,5,0,5,4,0,8,8,7,5,4,5,3,22
```

5.6 The problem with FOR ... NEXT

The FOR ... NEXT loop always executes at least once. It is not properly structured as it does not test the starting value, increment(or decrement), and finishing value to make sure that the loop should be entered. For example

FOR number = 6 TO 0 : PRINT number : NEXT number

would output 6. We would hopefully never write such bad code as this, but we might well want to code the next example.

```
430 FOR kount = start TO end STEP gap
440     PRINT kount
450 NEXT kount
```

Assuming that start contains 7.1, end contains 3.1 and gap contains 2.3, then the output from this loop will be

        7.1

when in fact we do not want any output.

When coding FOR loops, it is essential that we recognise those loops that could be executed zero times, and implement them in the following way.

```
420 IF (start - end ) * gap > 0 THEN GOTO 499
430 FOR kount = start TO end STEP gap
440     PRINT kount
450 NEXT kount
499 REM ENDLOOP 420
```

This implementation will work for any starting value, finishing value or increment/decrement; that is, any combination of positive and negative values. Note that the loop is executed if the starting and finishing values are the same.

A slight variation of this technique using procedures or subroutines is explained in chapter 7.

5.7 Summary of FOR

The FOR statement is powerful in BASIC but, because there is no test before entering the loop the first time, we have had to suggest a particular way of preserving structure and correct interpretation for the zero case.

There is an alternative approach using procedures or subroutines that are available on the BBC micro which will be discussed in chapter 7. However, procedures or subroutines are not available on all micros.

5.8 The REPEAT Statement

The REPEAT statement enables a sequence of instructions to be executed a number of times until a specified condition is true. The sequence of instructions is placed between the REPEAT statement and an UNTIL statement. For example

```
1000 REPEAT ...
1100
1200
1300
1400 UNTIL ...
```

We have seen, in design, that loops are needed which are executed while a particular condition is true. These are described as in figure 5.3.

(a)   7.1 LOOP while sum < 1000
        7.2   PRINT number
        7.3   sum=sum+number
        7.4   INPUT number
        7.5 ENDLOOP

(b)

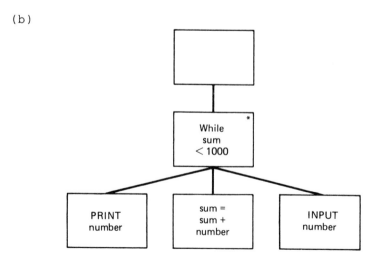

(c)

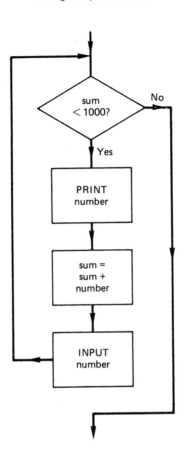

Figure 5.3

We need to examine the REPEAT ... UNTIL statement
very carefully in order to implement this design. For
example

```
10 sum = 0
20 INPUT "please enter a number",number
30 REPEAT
40    sum=sum + number
50    INPUT "please enter a number",number
60 UNTIL sum > 2000
70 PRINT sum
```

The code in lines 30 to 60 has set up a loop which is
executed a number of times, the exact number depending
on the numbers input. Thus, if 500, 501, 475, 525 are
entered, the output from this code is

2001

The code (lines 40 to 50) inside the loop is executed
once and then, until the condition is satisfied,
repeated again and again.

The actions that we wish to carry out are placed on
successive lines, but if the number of instructions is
small we can put the instructions one after the other
separated by a colon (:) up to the maximum line length
(230). For example

```
 5 INPUT number%
10 REPEAT
20      PRINT number%
30      PRINT number% * number%
40      INPUT number%
50 UNTIL number% < 0
```

can be coded as

```
 5 INPUT number%
10 REPEAT : PRINT number% : PRINT number% *  number%  :
INPUT number% : UNTIL number% < 0
```

These lines are multistatement lines and will thus
often exceed a single line on the screen. As already
mentioned, be careful not to press the RETURN key until
you have typed in the whole line. Again, indentation is
lost.
    If the numbers entered are 3, 4, 0, -1, the output
from this program is

```
        3
        9
        4
       16
        0
        0
```

The condition specified after UNTIL has exactly the
same format as the condition in an IF statement and can
thus be a numeric, alphanumeric or boolean test. The
operators AND, OR and EOR can also be used. For example

```
10 sum = 0
20 INPUT "please enter a number",number
30 REPEAT
40     sum=sum + number
50     INPUT "please enter a number",number
60 UNTIL sum > 2000 OR number < 0
70 PRINT sum
```

In this case the loop is terminated when either the sum > 2000 or a number < 0 has just been input.

Note that the condition UNTIL FALSE can be used to construct a forever loop. For example, the following code will print the time continuously

```
10 INPUT "what is the time in hrs,mins,secs,please",
    hrs,mins,secs
20  TIME =((hrs*60+mins)*60+secs)*100
30 REPEAT
40     secs=(TIME DIV 100) MOD 60
50     mins=(TIME DIV 6000) MOD 60
60     hrs=(TIME DIV 360000) MOD 24
70     PRINT "TIME NOW IS  ";hrs,mins,secs
80 UNTIL FALSE
```

5.9 Problems with REPEAT ... UNTIL
The REPEAT ... UNTIL is an example of a post conditioned UNTIL loop. That is, the coding in the loop is executed once and then the condition is tested; as long as the condition is not satisfied, the coding in the loop is then re-executed.

In design, the pre-conditioned "WHILE" loop is generally more convenient to use. Therefore it is necessary to translate pre-conditioned "WHILE" loops into post-conditioned REPEAT ... UNTIL loops. This is not difficult, except where on occasions we may not wish to enter the loop at all. For example

```
7.1 LOOP while sum < 1000
7.2     PRINT number
7.3     sum=sum+number
7.4     INPUT number
7.5 ENDLOOP
```

can be coded as

```
710 REPEAT
720     PRINT number
730     sum=sum+number
740     INPUT number
750 UNTIL sum >= 1000
```

All we have to do is to put the condition test at the end rather than at the beginning of the loop and reverse it. Be careful - for example, the opposite of < is >=.

When coding REPEAT loops it is essential that we recognise those loops that could be executed zero times and implement as in the following example.

```
700 IF sum >= 1000 THEN GOTO 799
710 REPEAT
720      PRINT number
730      sum=sum+number
740      INPUT number
750 UNTIL sum >= 1000
799 REM ENDLOOP 700
```

This implementation ensures that, before entering the
loop the first time, we make the same test as is made
on the UNTIL and jump over the loop altogether if the
condition is already satisfied. A slight variation of
this technique using procedures or subroutines is
explained in chapter 7.

5.10 Summary of REPEAT
The REPEAT statement is powerful in BASIC but, because
there is no test before entering the loop the first
time, we have had to suggest a particular way to
preserve structure and correct interpretation for the
zero case.

There is an alternative approach using procedures or
subroutines that are available on the BBC micro which
will be discussed in chapter 7. However, procedures or
subroutines are not available on all micros.

5.11 Summary
Provided that design has been carried out in sufficient
detail, coding for loops can become a purely mechanical
process if some of the implementations suggested above
are used in a consistent manner or if procedures or
subroutines are used as will be explained later in
chapter 7.

6 The Complete Program in BASIC

6.1 Introduction
In this chapter I have tried to illustrate, using a fairly simple programming problem, the principles of programming so far described. The specification, design and coding are thus shown in detail.

6.2 Specification
The specification for this problem is as follows.

(a) The results of an examination are to be processed to produce a report in the following format

```
 EXAM   REPORT
**************
QUESNO PERCENT
**************
CANDIDATE 1234
136      80.00
254      70.00
362      20.00 BELOW STANDARD
493      10.00 BELOW STANDARD
547      66.67
FAIL
***************
CANDIDATE 2643
262      80.00
349      60.00
263      80.00
728      93.33
543      96.67
PASS SECOND
**************
CANDIDATE 2948
126      60.00
648      60.00
379      60.00
328      60.00
349      70.00
PASS
**************
NUMBER OF CANDIDATES = 3
```

(b) Each candidate has a four-digit candidate number and this number is followed by five pairs of numbers, representing the question number and mark respectively for each question.

(c) Each question has a three-digit question number (in the range 100 to 999) and each mark is a two-digit number. Question numbers whose senior digit is 1 or 2 are marked out of 10, those whose senior digit is 3 are marked out of 20. All other questions are marked out of 30.

(d) The message "BELOW STANDARD" is printed alongside any question for which the candidate attained less than 50 per cent of the possible marks.

(e) A candidate fails the examination if any question is below standard or the averaged percentage does not exceed 60%. A candidate who passes the examination is classified as FIRST if the averaged percentage exceeds 90, SECOND if it exceeds 80 and THIRD if it exceeds 70.

(f) There is at least one candidate. The data is terminated by a candidate whose number is zero.

6.3 Program Design
This is as shown in figures 6.1, 6.2 and 6.3.

```
1.    Initialisation
2.    Processing
3.    Termination

1.2   Clear screen, Print 4 heading lines
1.3   Read first candidate's data

2.0    LOOP while candidate
2.1       add 1 to countcand%, zeroise
          totpercent
2.2       print candidate number and zeroise swfail%
2.3       process questions
2.4       calculate actual totpercent
2.5       establish grade
```

```
2.6      move to next line, print * line
2.7      read next candidate's data
2.9    ENDLOOP

3.1    Print number of candidates
3.2    End

2.30   LOOP tblpointer% from 1 to 5
2.31      print qno%
2.32      determine question percent in wkpercent
2.33      print wkpercent, add wkpercent to totpercent
2.34      determine standard
2.35      move to next print line
2.39   ENDLOOP

2.321  IF qno% is 400-999
2.3211 THEN calculate mark out of 30 in wkpercent
2.322  ELSEIF qno% is 300-399
2.3221 THEN calculate mark out of 20 in wkpercent
2.323  ELSE
2.3231      calculate mark out of 10 in wkpercent
2.329  ENDIF

2.3410 IF wkpercent < 50
2.3411 THEN Print "Below standard", set swfail%
2.349  ENDIF

2.51   IF totpercent <= 60 OR swfail% set
2.511  THEN print "fail"
2.52   ELSE
2.521       print "pass"
2.522       IF totpercent > 90
2.523       THEN print "first"
2.524       ELSEIF totpercent > 80
2.525       THEN print "second"
2.526       ELSEIF totpercent > 70
2.527       THEN print "third"
2.529       ENDIF
2.59   ENDIF
1.31   Read candidate%
1.320  LOOP tblpointer% from 1 to 5
1.321     Read qno%
1.322     Read mark%
1.329  ENDLOOP

2.71   Read candidate%
2.720  LOOP tblpointer% from 1 to 5
2.721     Read qno%
2.722     Read mark%
2.729  ENDLOOP
```

Figure 6.1

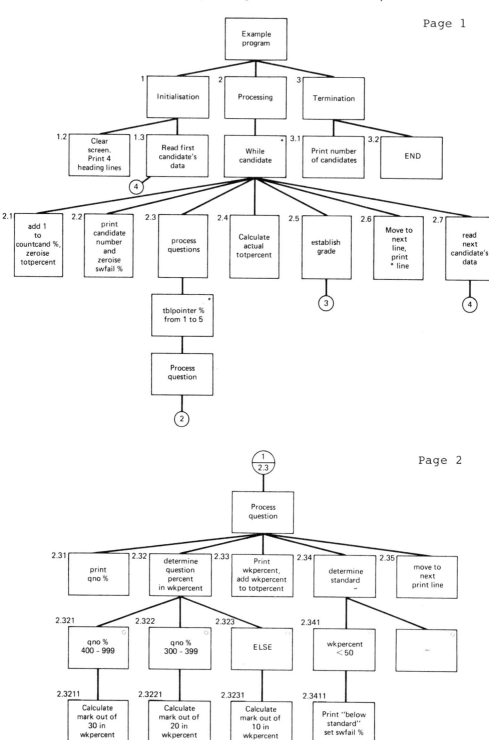

Page 1

Page 2

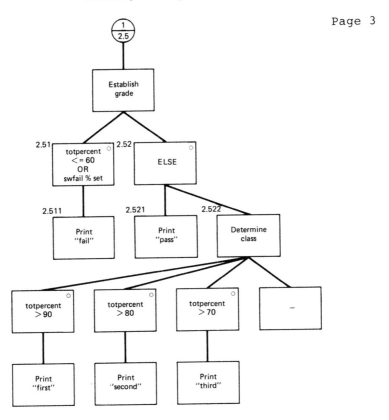

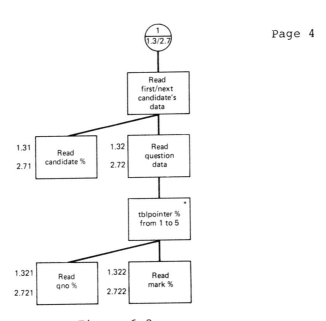

Figure 6.2

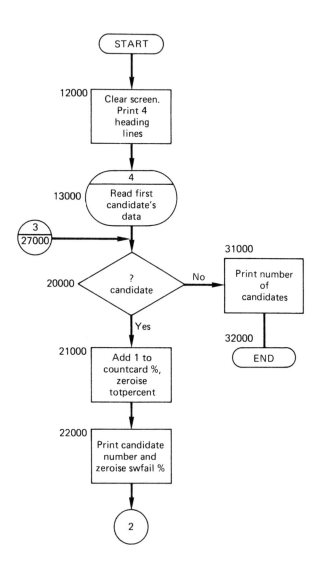

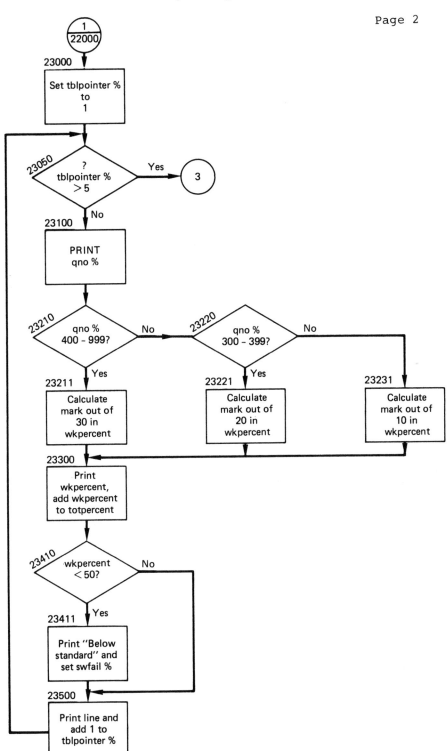

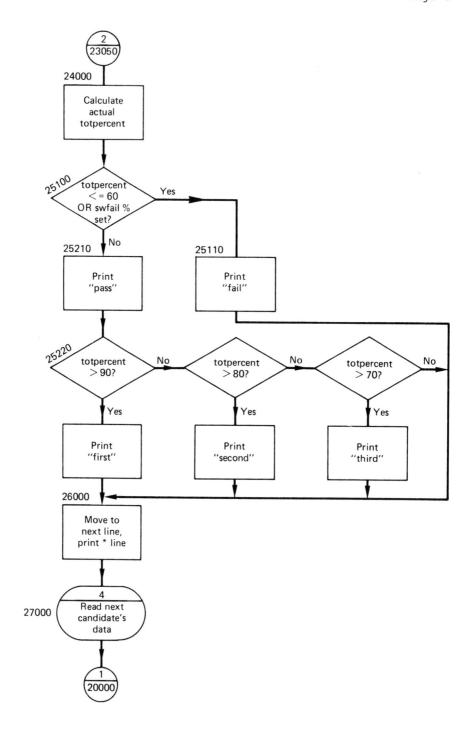

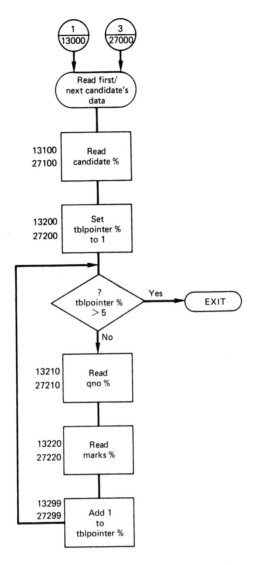

Figure 6.3

6.4 Coding
The coding for this program is shown in five different
ways, the latter versions showing some techniques that
you will meet later; they are included here for
completeness.

6.5 Coding (Without Subroutines or Procedures)
The first version of the program only uses instructions
that have been dealt with previously. When implementing
decisions, all IFs (except 25220) have been implemented

with GOTO after both THEN and ELSE, even if there is no action when the condition test is false. The IF at 25220 has been implemented as a single statement since there is only one action in each case and the maximum line length is not exceeded.

```
    2  REM   THIS IS AN EXAMPLE PROGRAM-CHAP6
    4  REM   The program starts at line 12000
    6  REM   The data is held in lines 10-360
   10 DATA 1234
   20 DATA 136,8
   30 DATA 254,7
   40 DATA 362,4
   50 DATA 493,3
   60 DATA 547,20
  110 DATA 2643
  120 DATA 262,8
  130 DATA 349,12
  140 DATA 263,8
  150 DATA 728,28
  160 DATA 543,29
  210 DATA 2948
  220 DATA 126,6
  230 DATA 648,18
  240 DATA 379,12
  250 DATA 328,12
  260 DATA 349,14
  310 DATA 0
  320 DATA 0,0
  330 DATA 0,0
  340 DATA 0,0
  350 DATA 0,0
  360 DATA 0,0
 9000   DIM qno%(5)
 9100   DIM marks%(5)
12000   CLS : PRINT " EXAM   REPORT " : PRINT
"**************" : PRINT "QUESNO PERCENT" : PRINT
"**************"
13100   READ candidate%
13200   FOR tblpointer% = 1 TO 5
13210     READ qno%(tblpointer%)
13220     READ marks%(tblpointer%)
13299   NEXT tblpointer%
20000   REPEAT
21000     countcand% = countcand% + 1 :
          totpercent = 0
22000     PRINT "CANDIDATE " , candidate% :
          swfail% = 0
23000     FOR tblpointer% = 1 TO 5
23100       PRINT qno%(tblpointer%);
```

```
23210      IF qno%(tblpointer%) > 399 THEN
           GOTO 23211 ELSE GOTO 23220
23211      wkpercent = (100 *
           marks%(tblpointer%)) / 30
23219        GOTO 23299
23220      IF qno%(tblpointer%) > 299 THEN GOTO 23221
           ELSE GOTO 23230
23221        wkpercent = 5 *
             marks%(tblpointer%)
23229        GOTO 23299
23230      REM DEFAULT
23231        wkpercent = 10 *
             marks%(tblpointer%)
23299      REM ENDIF 23210
23300      @% = &0002020A : PRINT wkpercent; : @% = &0
           : totpercent = totpercent + wkpercent
23410      IF wkpercent < 50 THEN GOTO 23411
           ELSE GOTO 23420
23411        PRINT " BELOW STANDARD"; : swfail% = 1
23419        GOTO 23499
23420      REM DEFAULT
23421        REM -
23499      REM ENDIF 23410
23500        PRINT
23999    NEXT tblpointer%
24000    totpercent = totpercent / 5
25100    IF totpercent <= 60 OR swfail% = 1 THEN
         GOTO 25110 ELSE GOTO 25200
25110      PRINT "FAIL ";
25199      GOTO 25999
25200    REM DEFAULT
25210      PRINT "PASS ";
25220      IF totpercent > 90 THEN PRINT "FIRST";
           ELSE IF totpercent > 80 THEN PRINT "SECOND";
           ELSE IF totpercent > 70 THEN PRINT "THIRD";

25999    REM ENDIF 25100
26000    PRINT : PRINT "**************"
27100    READ candidate%
27200    FOR tblpointer% = 1 TO 5
27210      READ qno%(tblpointer%)
27220      READ marks%(tblpointer%)
27299    NEXT tblpointer%
29999  UNTIL candidate% = 0
31000  PRINT "NUMBER OF CANDIDATES = " , countcand%
32000  END
```

6.6 Coding (Using One Subroutine)
The second version of the program uses a subroutine,
the details of which will be met in chapter 7. The
only differences between this and the previous version

will be found on lines 5, 1100 to 1999, 13000 to 13299 and 27000 to 27299.

A subroutine has been defined in lines 1100 to 1999 and the code in that subroutine has been deleted from both lines 13100 to 13299 and 27100 to 27299. At each of these two points (13000 and 27000) a call to the subroutine has been introduced.

A GOTO is required in line 5 to jump over the subroutine when the program starts; the subroutine could alternatively be defined at the physical end of the program.

```
   2   REM   THIS IS AN EXAMPLE PROGRAM-CHAP6G
   4   REM   The program starts at line 12000
   5   GOTO 9000
   6   REM   The data is held in lines 10-360
  10 DATA 1234
  20 DATA 136,8
  30 DATA 254,7
  40 DATA 362,4
  50 DATA 493,3
  60 DATA 547,20
 110 DATA 2643
 120 DATA 262,8
 130 DATA 349,12
 140 DATA 263,8
 150 DATA 728,28
 160 DATA 543,29
 210 DATA 2948
 220 DATA 126,6
 230 DATA 648,18
 240 DATA 379,12
 250 DATA 328,12
 260 DATA 349,14
 310 DATA 0
 320 DATA 0,0
 330 DATA 0,0
 340 DATA 0,0
 350 DATA 0,0
 360 DATA 0,0
1100   READ candidate%
1200   FOR tblpointer% = 1 TO 5
1210     READ qno%(tblpointer%)
1220     READ marks%(tblpointer%)
1299   NEXT tblpointer%
1999   RETURN : REM ENTRY AT 1100
9000   DIM qno%(5)
9100   DIM marks%(5)
12000   CLS : PRINT " EXAM  REPORT " : PRINT
"**************" : PRINT "QUESNO PERCENT" : PRINT
"***************"
```

```
13000   GOSUB 1100 :REM READ A RECORD
20000   REPEAT
21000     countcand% = countcand% + 1 : totpercent = 0
22000     PRINT "CANDIDATE " , candidate% : swfail% = 0
23000     FOR tblpointer% = 1 TO 5
23100       PRINT qno%(tblpointer%);
23210       IF qno%(tblpointer%) > 399 THEN GOTO 23211
            ELSE GOTO 23220
23211         wkpercent = (100 * marks%(tblpointer%))
              / 30
23219         GOTO 23299
23220       IF qno%(tblpointer%) > 299 THEN GOTO 23221
            ELSE GOTO 23230
23221         wkpercent = 5 * marks%(tblpointer%)
23229         GOTO 23299
23230       REM DEFAULT
23231         wkpercent = 10 * marks%(tblpointer%)
23299       REM ENDIF 23210
23300       @% = &0002020A : PRINT wkpercent; : @% = &0
            : totpercent = totpercent + wkpercent
23410       IF wkpercent < 50 THEN GOTO 23411
            ELSE GOTO 23420
23411         PRINT " BELOW STANDARD"; : swfail% = 1
23419         GOTO 23499
23420       REM DEFAULT
23421         REM -
23499       REM ENDIF 23410
23500       PRINT
23999     NEXT tblpointer%
24000     tctpercent = totpercent / 5
25100     IF totpercent <= 60 OR swfail% = 1 THEN
          GOTO 25110 ELSE GOTO 25200
25110       PRINT "FAIL ";
25199       GOTO 25999
25200     REM DEFAULT
25210       PRINT "PASS ";
25220       IF totpercent > 90 THEN PRINT "FIRST";
            ELSE IF totpercent > 80 THEN PRINT "SECOND";
            ELSE IF totpercent > 70 THEN PRINT "THIRD";
25999     REM ENDIF 25100
26000     PRINT : PRINT "**************"
27000     GOSUB 1100 :REM READ A RECORD
29999   UNTIL candidate% = 0
31000   PRINT "NUMBER OF CANDIDATES = " , countcand%
32000   END
```

6.7 Coding (Using One Procedure)

The third version of the program uses a procedure that will also be met in chapter 7. The only differences between this and the first version will be found on lines 5, 1000 to 1999, 13000 to 13299 and 27000 to 27299.

A procedure has been defined in lines 1000 to 1999 and the code in that procedure has been deleted from both lines 13100 to 13299 and 27100 to 27299. At each of these two points (13000 and 27000) a call to the procedure has been introduced.

A GOTO is required in line 5 to jump over the procedure when the program starts; the procedure could alternatively be defined at the physical end of the program.

To convert the subroutine in the second version to a procedure in the third version required only three changes:

Replace RETURN with ENDPROC
Introduce DEF PROCreadrecord at the beginning of the module code
Replace GOSUBs with PROCreadrecord

```
   2  REM  THIS IS AN EXAMPLE PROGRAM-CHAP6M1
   4  REM  The program starts at line 12000
   5  GOTO 9000
   6  REM  The data is held in lines 10-360
  10  DATA 1234
  20  DATA 136,8
  30  DATA 254,7
  40  DATA 362,4
  50  DATA 493,3
  60  DATA 547,20
 110  DATA 2643
 120  DATA 262,8
 130  DATA 349,12
 140  DATA 263,8
 150  DATA 728,28
 160  DATA 543,29
 210  DATA 2948
 220  DATA 126,6
 230  DATA 648,18
 240  DATA 379,12
 250  DATA 328,12
 260  DATA 349,14
 310  DATA 0
 320  DATA 0,0
 330  DATA 0,0
 340  DATA 0,0
 350  DATA 0,0
 360  DATA 0,0
1000  DEF PROCreadrecord
1100  READ candidate%
1200  FOR tblpointer% = 1 TO 5
```

```
 1210     READ qno%(tblpointer%)
 1220     READ marks%(tblpointer%)
 1299   NEXT tblpointer%
 1999   ENDPROC : REM FROM 1000
 9000   DIM qno%(5)
 9100   DIM marks%(5)
12000   CLS : PRINT " EXAM  REPORT " : PRINT
"**************" : PRINT "QUESNO PERCENT" : PRINT
"**************"
13000   PROCreadrecord
20000   REPEAT
21000     countcand% = countcand% + 1 : totpercent = 0
22000     PRINT "CANDIDATE " , candidate% : swfail% = 0
23000     FOR tblpointer% = 1 TO 5
23100       PRINT qno%(tblpointer%);
23210       IF qno%(tblpointer%) > 399 THEN GOTO 23211
            ELSE GOTO 23220
23211         wkpercent = (100 * marks%(tblpointer%))
              / 30
23219         GOTO 23299
23220       IF qno%(tblpointer%) > 299 THEN GOTO 23221
            ELSE GOTO 23230
23221         wkpercent = 5 * marks%(tblpcinter%)
23229         GOTO 23299
23230       REM DEFAULT
23231         wkpercent = 10 * marks%(tblpointer%)
23299       REM ENDIF 23210
23300       @% = &0002020A : PRINT wkpercent; : @% = &0
            : totpercent = totpercent + wkpercent
23410       IF wkpercent < 50 THEN GOTO 23411
            ELSE GOTO 23420
23411         PRINT " BELOW STANDARD"; : swfail% = 1
23419         GOTO 23499
23420       REM DEFAULT
23421         REM -
23499       REM ENDIF 23410
23500       PRINT
23999     NEXT tblpointer%
24000     totpercent = totpercent / 5
25100     IF totpercent <= 60 OR swfail% = 1 THEN
          GOTO 25110 ELSE GOTO 25200
25110       PRINT "FAIL ";
25199       GOTO 25999
25200     REM DEFAULT
25210       PRINT "PASS ";
25220       IF totpercent > 90 THEN PRINT "FIRST";
            ELSE IF totpercent > 80 THEN PRINT "SECOND";
            ELSE IF totpercent > 70 THEN PRINT "THIRD";
25999     REM ENDIF 25100
26000     PRINT : PRINT "**************"
27000   PROCreadrecord
```

```
29999  UNTIL candidate% = 0
31000  PRINT "NUMBER OF CANDIDATES = " , countcand%
32000  END
```

6.8 Coding (Using Many Procedures)

This fourth version of the program uses procedures
that, once again, will be met in chapter 7. The
procedure readrecord has been retained and three
further procedures, processrecord, processquestion and
establishgrade, have been introduced. Note that it is
now necessary to change the line numbers on GOTOs in
the procedures.

```
   2 REM   THIS IS AN EXAMPLE PROGRAM-CHAP6M2
   4 REM   The program starts at line 12000
   5 GOTO 9000
   6 REM   The data is held in lines 10-360
  10 DATA 1234
  20 DATA 136,8
  30 DATA 254,7
  40 DATA 362,4
  50 DATA 493,3
  60 DATA 547,20
 110 DATA 2643
 120 DATA 262,8
 130 DATA 349,12
 140 DATA 263,8
 150 DATA 728,28
 160 DATA 543,29
 210 DATA 2948
 220 DATA 126,6
 230 DATA 648,18
 240 DATA 379,12
 250 DATA 328,12
 260 DATA 349,14
 310 DATA 0
 320 DATA 0,0
 330 DATA 0,0
 340 DATA 0,0
 350 DATA 0,0
 360 DATA 0,0
1000 DEF PROCreadrecord
1100 READ candidate%
1200 FOR tblpointer% = 1 TO 5
1210    READ qno%(tblpointer%)
1220    READ marks%(tblpointer%)
1299 NEXT tblpointer%
1999 ENDPROC : REM FROM 1000
2000 DEF PROCprocessrecord
2100 countcand% = countcand% + 1 : totpercent = 0
```

```
2200 PRINT "CANDIDATE " , candidate% : swfail% = 0
2300 FOR tblpointer% = 1 TO 5
2310    PROCprocessquestion
2399 NEXT tblpointer%
2400 totpercent = totpercent / 5
2500 PROCestablishgrade
2600 PRINT : PRINT "**************"
2700 PROCreadrecord
2999 ENDPROC : REM FROM 2000
3000 DEF PROCprocessquestion
3100 PRINT qno%(tblpointer%);
3210 IF qno%(tblpointer%) > 399 THEN GOTO 3211
     ELSE GOTO 3220
3211    wkpercent = (100 * marks%(tblpointer%)) / 30
3219    GOTO 3299
3220 IF qno%(tblpointer%) > 299 THEN GOTO 3221
     ELSE GOTO 3230
3221    wkpercent = 5 * marks%(tblpointer%)
3229    GOTO 3299
3230 REM DEFAULT
3231    wkpercent = 10 * marks%(tblpointer%)
3299 REM ENDIF 3210
3300 @% = &0002020A : PRINT wkpercent; : @% = &0 :
     totpercent = totpercent + wkpercent
3410 IF wkpercent < 50 THEN GOTO 3411 ELSE GOTO 3420
3411    PRINT " BELOW STANDARD"; : swfail% = 1
3419    GOTO 3499
3420 REM DEFAULT
3421    REM -
3499 REM ENDIF 3410
3500 PRINT
3999 ENDPROC : REM FROM 3000
5000 DEF PROCestablishgrade
5100 IF totpercent <= 60 OR swfail% = 1 THEN GOTO 5110
     ELSE GOTO 5200
5110    PRINT "FAIL ";
5199    GOTO 5999
5200 REM DEFAULT
5210    PRINT "PASS ";
5220    IF totpercent > 90 THEN PRINT "FIRST";
           ELSE IF totpercent > 80 THEN PRINT "SECOND";
           ELSE IF totpercent > 70 THEN PRINT "THIRD";
5999 ENDPROC  :REM FROM 5000 .ENDIF 5100
9000 DIM qno%(5)
9100 DIM marks%(5)
12000 CLS : PRINT " EXAM  REPORT " :
      PRINT "**************" : PRINT "QUESNO PERCENT" :
      PRINT "**************"
13000 PROCreadrecord
20000 REPEAT
21000    PROCprocessrecord
```

```
29999 UNTIL candidate% = 0
31000 PRINT "NUMBER OF CANDIDATES = " , countcand%
32000 END
```

6.9 Coding (Using Many Procedures and Using IF in Several Ways)

In the fifth version, the procedures have been retained but the IF statement has been, in my opinion, better used as follows. Where a single statement is required when a condition is true, it has been incorporated into the IF (6100). Where processing is required only if the condition is true, the ELSE clause has been omitted (3410). Where the processing required on a true or false path does not require a selection or iteration and the maximum line length is not exceeded, a multistatement line is used (3410 and 5100). Where a further selection or iteration is required or the maximum line length would be exceeded, a procedure is used (5100).

```
   2 REM   THIS IS AN EXAMPLE PROGRAM-CHAP6IF
   4 REM   The program starts at line 12000
   5 GOTO 9000
   6 REM   The data is held in lines 10-360
  10 DATA 1234
  20 DATA 136,8
  30 DATA 254,7
  40 DATA 362,4
  50 DATA 493,3
  60 DATA 547,20
 110 DATA 2643
 120 DATA 262,8
 130 DATA 349,12
 140 DATA 263,8
 150 DATA 728,28
 160 DATA 543,29
 210 DATA 2948
 220 DATA 126,6
 230 DATA 648,18
 240 DATA 379,12
 250 DATA 328,12
 260 DATA 349,14
 310 DATA 0
 320 DATA 0,0
 330 DATA 0,0
 340 DATA 0,0
 350 DATA 0,0
 360 DATA 0,0
1000 DEF PROCreadrecord
1100 READ candidate%
```

```
1200 FOR tblpointer% = 1 TO 5
1210   READ qno%(tblpointer%)
1220   READ marks%(tblpointer%)
1299 NEXT tblpointer%
1999 ENDPROC
2000 DEF PROCprocessrecord
2100 countcand% = countcand% + 1 : totpercent = 0
2200 PRINT "CANDIDATE " , candidate% : swfail% = 0
2300 FOR tblpointer% = 1 TO 5
2310   PROCprocessquestion
2399 NEXT tblpointer%
2400 totpercent = totpercent / 5
2500 PROCestablishgrade
2600 PRINT : PRINT "**************"
2700 PROCreadrecord
2999 ENDPROC
3000 DEF PROCprocessquestion
3100 PRINT qno%(tblpointer%);
3210 IF qno%(tblpointer%) > 399 THEN PROCout30
     ELSE IF qno%(tblpointer%) > 299 THEN PROCout20
     ELSE PROCout10
3300 @% = &0002020A : PRINT wkpercent; : @% = &0 :
     totpercent = totpercent + wkpercent
3410 IF wkpercent < 50 THEN PRINT " BELOW STANDARD"; :
     swfail% =1
3500 PRINT
3999 ENDPROC
5000 DEF PROCestablishgrade
5100 IF totpercent <= 60 OR swfail% = 1 THEN
     PRINT "FAIL "; ELSE PRINT "PASS ";  : PROCclass
5999 ENDPROC
6000 DEF PROCclass
6100 IF totpercent > 90 THEN PRINT "FIRST";
     ELSE IF totpercent > 80 THEN PRINT "SECOND";
     ELSE IF totpercent > 70 THEN PRINT "THIRD";
6999 ENDPROC
7100 DEF PROCout30
7110 wkpercent = (100 * marks%(tblpointer%)) / 30
7199 ENDPROC
7200 DEF PROCout20
7210 wkpercent = 5 * marks%(tblpointer%)
7299 ENDPROC
7300 DEF PROCout10
7310 wkpercent = 10 * marks% tblpointer%)
7399   ENDPROC
9000 DIM qno%(5)
9100 DIM marks%(5)
12000 CLS : PRINT " EXAM  REPORT " :
      PRINT "**************" : PRINT "QUESNO PERCENT" :
      PRINT "**************"
13000 PROCreadrecord
```

```
20000 REPEAT
21000    PROCprocessrecord
29999 UNTIL candidate% = 0
31000 PRINT "NUMBER OF CANDIDATES = " , countcand%
32000 END
```

6.10 Testing, Implementation and Review

Testing, implementation and review would be needed for
this program, but the details of these processes will
be dealt with later.

6.11 Summary

The program design was relatively easy since the
specification was comprehensive. Different forms of
selections and iterations were deliberately included so
that their incorporation into a complete design and
their subsequent coding could be seen.

  For the BBC microcomputer, I prefer the last version
of the code; that is, where procedures are liberally
used and the IF statement is used in four different but
consistent ways.

  On other micros, procedures may not be available and
subroutines should be used instead. In some cases the
IF is not implemented in such a flexible way and the
first version may be the only one possible.

  REPEAT ... UNTIL is not always available and the WHILE
loop should, in this case, be coded using IF and GOTO.
I would always choose to code it in the following
symbolic manner:

```
        loopstartnumber IF NOT (whilecondition)
                        GOTO nextstatement
                        . . . .
                        . . . .
                        . . . .
        loopreturnnumber GOTO loopstartnumber
        nextstatement    . . . .
```

7 Modules

7.1 Introduction
Modular programming is used to break down a large program into smaller parts for easier design and coding. It is also useful for isolating a routine that can be of use in more than one place in a program, or in more than one program, and enables a number of programmers to work on the same program at the same time.

A module is not just a sequence of program code conveniently placed together; it must be a logical entity within an overall design.

Suppose that we need the following five lines of code to obtain eleven items of data concerning a particular candidate. In our design it is probably just stated as "obtain next candidate's data", but this statement appears in more than one place so the five lines have to be repeated each time.

```
READ candidate%
FOR tblpointer% = 1 TO 5
  READ qno%(tblpointer%)
  READ marks%(tblpointer%)
NEXT tblpointer%
```

We can easily convert this into a subroutine or procedure, as we shall see in a moment.

7.2 Subroutines (GOSUB and RETURN)
There are only three operations that we must carry out if we choose to use a subroutine rather than include the necessary instructions directly.

The first operation is to place the instructions themselves where they will not be directly executed; that is, after the logical END statement, or at the beginning of the program before any DIM statements or the first logical instruction, in which case a GOTO is necessary at the physical beginning of the program to jump to the first DIM or logical instruction. For example

```
    either
    .....
    .....    Program logic
    .....
    END
    .....
    .....    Subroutine
    .....

    or

    GOTO 5000
    .....
    .....    Subroutine
    .....
5000 DIM names$(8)
5100 .....
5200 .....
5300 .....    Program logic
5400 .....
5500 END
```

The second operation is to add a RETURN line after the last instruction in the subroutine. For example

```
1100 READ candidate%
1200 FOR tblpointer% = 1 TO 5
1210    READ qno%(tblpointer%)
1220    READ marks%(tblpointer%)
1299 NEXT tblpointer%
1999 RETURN : REM ENTRY AT 1100
```

I always include a comment after the RETURN statement so that I know where the subroutine began. It is useful when you have several subroutines grouped together.

The third operation is to include in the program logic itself a GOSUB statement wherever the code in the subroutine would otherwise have been placed. This GOSUB must state the line number on which the subroutine begins. For example

```
7000 GOSUB 1100 : REM - obtain candidate data
```

When this GOSUB statement is executed, control is passed to the line number specified (in this case 1100) and continues from that point until RETURN is met, when control is passed to the next line number after the GOSUB statement (in this case the next line number after 7000). It is a good idea to add a comment about the processing carried out in the subroutine after the GOSUB statement, as shown in the example.

7.3 Procedures (DEF PROC and ENDPROC)
As with subroutines, there are only three operations that we must carry out if we choose to use a procedure rather than include the necessary instructions directly.

The first operation is to place the instructions themselves where they will not be directly executed; after the logical END statement, or at the beginning of the program before any DIM statements or the first logical instruction, in which case a GOTO is necessary at the physical beginning of the program to jump to the first DIM or logical instruction. For example

```
        either
        .....
        .....      Program logic
        .....
        END
        .....
        .....      Procedure
        .....

        or

        GOTO 5000
        .....
        .....      Procedure
        .....
5000 DIM names$(8)
5100 .....
5200 .....
5300 .....      Program logic
5400 .....
5500 END
```

The second operation is to add a DEF PROC statement (which gives the procedure a name) before the first instruction in the procedure, and an ENDPROC statement after the last instruction in the procedure. For example

```
1000 DEF PROCreadrecord
1100 READ candidate%
1200 FOR tblpointer% = 1 TO 5
1210    READ qno%(tblpointer%)
1220    READ marks%(tblpointer%)
1299 NEXT tblpointer%
1999 ENDPROC : REM FROM 1000
```

I always include a comment after the ENDPROC statement so that I know where the procedure began. It is useful when you have several procedures grouped together.

The third operation is to include in the program logic itself the procedure name wherever the code in the procedure would otherwise have been placed. Because the name rather than a line number is used, a program with procedures is easier to read than one with subroutines.

7000 PROCreadrecord

When this procedure name is met, control is passed to the procedure specified and continues from that point until ENDPROC is met, when control is passed to the next line number after the procedure name (in this case the next line number after 7000).

A number of procedures have been used in the last version of the example program in chapter 6.

7.4 Procedures with Parameters
BBC BASIC allows parameters to be passed to a procedure by a technique known as "call by value". Here are a few examples to illustrate the technique.

Suppose that we need a procedure to print a line of asterisks and then move to the next line. The problem is that the required number of asterisks varies. For instance, sometimes we need a line of ten asterisks.

* * * * * * * * * *

and sometimes we need three asterisks

* * *

Consider this short program:

```
 10  PROCstar(10)
 20  no=3
 30  PROCstar(no)
 40  END
100  DEF PROCstar(x)
200  FOR count = 1 TO x
300    PRINT "*";
400  NEXT count
500  PRINT
600  ENDPROC : REM FROM 100
```

We have defined a procedure called star but this time, after the name, we have written (x). The round brackets indicate a list of one or more "formal parameters", in this case one called x. Notice that in the body of the procedure x is used to control the limit of the FOR loop. When we call the procedure (in lines 10 and 30) we must either specify a value which is transferred into x at the beginning of the procedure or the name of a variable whose contents are copied into x at the beginning of the procedure.

Thus the output from the above program is

```
**********
***
```

Consider a second example:

```
 10  christianname$="JOHN"
 20  surname$="SMITH"
 30  PROCadds(christianname$,surname$)
 40  PRINT newname$
 50  END
100  DEF PROCadds(f$,s$)
200  newname$ = f$ + " " + s$
300  ENDPROC : REM FROM 100
```

In this example we have two formal parameters, f$ and s$. When the procedure is called in line 30, the contents of christianname$ (JOHN) will be transferred into f$ and the contents of surname$ (SMITH) will be transferred into s$. Thus in line 200 the string JOHN SMITH is transferred into newname$ and the output from the program (from line 40) is

JOHN SMITH

Note that the formal parameters "exist" only during the execution of the procedure, and it is not possible to pass values back from the procedure to the main logic. Therefore the following program, intended to swap the contents of two stores, does **not** work!

```
christianname$="SMITH"
surname$="JOHN"
PROCswap(christianname$,surname$)
PRINT christianname$," ",surname$
END
DEF PROCswap(f$,s$)
w$=f$
f$=s$
s$=w$
ENDPROC : REM FROM ???
```

This program does not work because the swapping is
carried out between f$ and s$; the actual parameters
christianname$ and surname$ are unchanged.
    The following procedure (without parameters) on
lines 100 to 500 would achieve the desired purpose, but
further similar procedures would be needed to swap any
stores other than christianname$ and surname$.

```
 10 christianname$="SMITH"
 20 surname$="JOHN"
 30 PROCswap
 40 PRINT christianname$;" ";surname$
 50 END
100 DEF PROCswap
200 w$=christianname$
300 christianname$=surname$
400 surname$=w$
500 ENDPROC : REM FROM 100
```

The output from the program(line 40) is
JOHN SMITH

7.5 Procedures with LOCAL Variables
Let us take another look at the program that produces
lines of asterisks. I have added two lines, a FOR and a
NEXT around the procedure calls, so that I get my two
lines of asterisks six times. But the program does not
stop!

```
FOR count% = 1 TO 6
    PROCstar(10)
    no%=3
    PROCstar(no%)
  NEXT count%
  END
  DEF PROCstar(x)
  FOR count% = 1 TO x
      PRINT "*";
  NEXT count%
  PRINT
  ENDPROC : REM FROM 100
```

This is because I am using the variable count to
control the number of times that I repeat the two
lines, and also to control the number of asterisks on
the line. Now if I was writing the whole program myself
I would keep a data table and make sure that I used a
different name in my procedure. But suppose that
someone else is writing the procedure. We can make sure
that a new variable called count is used in the

procedure by adding a LOCAL line between the heading and the body of the procedure, thus:

```
  5 FOR count% = 1 TO 6
 10     PROCstar(10)
 20     no%=3
 30     PROCstar(no%)
 35 NEXT count%
 40 END
100 DEF PROCstar(x)
150 LOCAL count%
200 FOR count% = 1 TO x
300     PRINT "*";
400 NEXT count%
500 PRINT
600 ENDPROC : REM FROM 100
```

The successful output from this program is

```
**********
***
**********
***
**********
***
**********
***
**********
***
**********
***
```

7.6 Implementing Decisions Using IF

There were two problems encountered in chapter 4 with IF ... THEN ... and IF ... THEN ... ELSE when implementing decisions. Firstly, what happens when the IF statement needed exceeds the maximum line length? Secondly, is it not possible to preserve the indentation used in design?

These two problems can be overcome by using procedures or subroutines. For example, the design

```
2.1    IF mark larger than 50
2.105  THEN
2.11       PRINT "PASS"
2.12       p=p+1
2.2    ELSE
2.21       PRINT "FAIL"
2.22       f=f+1
2.9    ENDIF
```

could be coded (using procedures) as

```
2100 IF mark > 50 THEN PROCpass ELSE PROCfail
...............
...............
4000 END
5000 DEF PROCpass
5110    PRINT "PASS"
5120    p = p + 1
5199 ENDPROC : REM FROM 5000
5200 DEF PROCfail
5210    PRINT "FAIL"
5220    f = f + 1
5299 ENDPROC : REM FROM 5200
```

It could also be coded (using subroutines) as

```
2100 IF mark > 50 THEN GOSUB 5110 ELSE GOSUB 5210
...............
4000 END
5110    PRINT "PASS"
5120    p = p + 1
5199 RETURN : REM ENTRY AT 5110
5210    PRINT "FAIL"
5220    f = f + 1
5299 RETURN : REM ENTRY AT 5210
```

Indentation is thus preserved and multistatement lines
are avoided. The maximum line length can be exceeded
for a very long condition!
   Also the design

```
2.1    IF mark larger than 50
2.105 THEN
2.11      PRINT "PASS"
2.12      p=p+1
2.2    ELSEIF mark  larger than 30
2.205 THEN
2.21      PRINT "FAIL"
2.22      f=f+1
2.3    ELSE
2.31      PRINT "BAD FAIL"
2.32      b=b+1
2.9    ENDIF
```

could be coded (using procedures) as

```
2100  IF mark > 50 THEN PROCpass ELSE IF mark > 30 THEN
PROCfail ELSE PROCbadfail....................
...................
...................
4000 END
```

```
5105 DEF PROCpass
5110    PRINT "PASS"
5120    p = p + 1
5199 ENDPROC : REM FROM 5105
5200 DEF PROCfail
5210    PRINT "FAIL"
5220    f = f + 1
5299 ENDPROC : REM FROM 5200
5300 DEF PROCbadfail
5310    PRINT "BAD FAIL"
5320    b = b + 1
5999 ENDPROC : REM FROM 5300
```

It could, in addition, be coded (using subroutines) as

```
2100 IF mark > 50 THEN GOSUB 5110 ELSE  IF  mark  >   30
THEN GOSUB 5210 ELSE GOSUB 5310
............
............
4000 END
5110    PRINT "PASS"
5120    p = p + 1
5199 RETURN : REM FROM 5110
5210    PRINT "FAIL"
5220    f = f + 1
5299 RETURN : REM FROM 5210
5310    PRINT "BAD FAIL"
5320    b = b + 1
5999 RETURN : REM FROM 5310
```

The layout for IF ... THEN ... will be more like top-down if we code using procedures or subroutines. For instance, the design

```
2.1    IF mark larger than 50
2.105 THEN
2.11      PRINT "PASS"
2.12      p=p+1
2.9    ENDIF
```

could be coded (using procedures) as

```
2100 IF mark > 50 THEN PROCpass
...............
...............
4000 END
5000 DEF PROCpass
5110    PRINT "PASS"
5120    p = p + 1
5199 ENDPROC : REM FROM 5000
```

It could also be coded (using subroutines) as

```
2100 IF mark > 50 THEN GOSUB 5110
..............
4000 END
5110    PRINT "PASS"
5120    p = p + 1
5199 RETURN : REM ENTRY AT 5110
```

Indentation is thus also preserved and multistatement lines are avoided. The maximum line length can also be exceeded for a very long condition!

We found previously that it was possible to use IF immediately after THEN and also after ELSE, but extreme care must be exercised when doing this.

Consider again one of the structures that gave trouble.

```
        IF month = 11
        THEN
            IF day = 5
            THEN
                PRINT "BONFIRE NIGHT"
            ELSE
                PRINT "WRONG DAY"
            ENDIF
        ELSE
            PRINT "WRONG MONTH"
        ENDIF
```

This could be successfully coded (using procedures) by calling a procedure at each level, such as

```
21000 IF month =11 THEN PROC11
      ELSE PROCnot11
.............
.............
24000 END
25000 DEF PROC11
25100 IF day = 5 THEN PROC5
      ELSE PROCnot5
25103 ENDPROC : REM FROM 25100
25105    DEF PROC5
25110         PRINT "BONFIRE NIGHT"
25199    ENDPROC : REM FROM 25105
25200    DEF PROCnot5
25210         PRINT "WRONG DAY"
25999    ENDPROC : REM FROM 25200
26000 DEF PROCnot11
26100    PRINT "WRONG MONTH"
26999 ENDPROC : REM FROM 26000
```

This uses procedures at each level. However, there
is no need to use procedures at the lowest level,
therefore PROC5 and PROCnot5 need not be used. The
instructions can be incorporated into the IF directly,
as follows.

```
21000 IF month =11 THEN PROC11
      ELSE PROCnot11
. . . . . . . . . . . . . .
. . . . . . . . . . . . . .
24000 END
25000 DEF PROC11
25100 IF day  =  5  THEN  PRINT  "BONFIRE  NIGHT"  ELSE
PRINT"WRONG DAY"
25103 ENDPROC : REM FROM 25100
26000 DEF PROCnot11
26100     PRINT "WRONG MONTH"
26999 ENDPROC : REM FROM 26000
```

In fact, PROCnot11 is also unnecessary, the PRINT
statement could come after the ELSE. Strictly a
procedure is necessary only when we want a further IF
... THEN ... ELSE within the THEN part of an IF.
    This structure can also be coded using subroutines.
For example

```
21000 IF month =11 THEN GOSUB 25100
      ELSE GOSUB 26100
. . . . . . . . . . . . . .
. . . . . . . . . . . . . .
24000 END
25100     IF day = 5 THEN GOSUB 25110
          ELSE GOSUB 25210
25105     RETURN : REM ENTRY AT 25100
25110         PRINT "BONFIRE NIGHT"
25199         RETURN : REM ENTRY AT 25110
25210         PRINT "WRONG DAY"
25999         RETURN : REM ENTRY AT 25210
26100     PRINT "WRONG MONTH"
26999     RETURN : REM ENTRY AT 26100
```

Again, the only necessary subroutine is the one at
25100, the other three subroutines could have been
coded directly as PRINT statements after THEN or ELSE,
as appropriate. That is

```
21000 IF month =11 THEN GOSUB 25100
      ELSE PRINT "WRONG MONTH"
. . . . . . . . . . . . . .
. . . . . . . . . . . . . .
24000 END
```

```
25100     IF day = 5 THEN PRINT "BONFIRE  NIGHT" ELSE
PRINT "WRONG DAY"
25105     RETURN : REM ENTRY AT 25100
```

However, indentation is lost where procedures or subroutines are not consistently used.

The method whereby we can overcome a complicated condition exceeding the maximum line length (by splitting it into several conditions) is unchanged. We can use either a procedure cr a subroutine for each part of the test.

There are several ways in which IF can be used. Where a single statement is required when a condition is true, it can be directly incorporated into the IF. Where processing is required only if the condition is true, the ELSE clause can be omitted. Where the processing required on a true or false path does not require a selection or iteration and the maximum line length is not exceeded, a multistatement line can be used. Where a further selection or iteration is required or the maximum line length would be exceeded, a procedure or subroutine can be used. Examples of most of these can be seen in the fifth version of the program in section 6.8.

7.7 Implementing Decisions Using ON
The format

ON expression GOSUB ... ELSE ...

allows a jump to be made to one of a number of subroutines, depending on the value of the expression. For example

70 ON recordtype% GOSUB 500,600,200,500

means jump to linenumber 500 if recordtype is 1 or 4, to 600 if recordtype is 2, or to 200 if recordtype is 3, returning to the next higher line number (in this case after 70) when RETURN is met.

This represents the design shown in figure 7.1.

```
(a)    CASE recordtype is 1 or 4
            process A
       CASE recordtype is 2
            process B
       CASE recordtype is 3
            process C
       ENDCASE
```

(b)

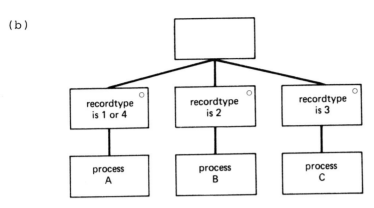

(c)

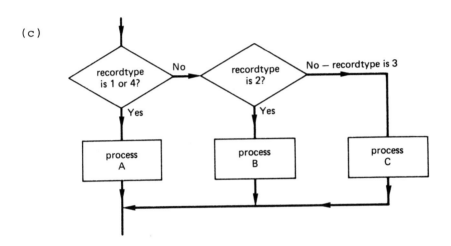

Figure 7.1

Here process A is coded at line 500, process B at 600, and process C at 200.

But what happens if recordtype is not 1, 2, 3 or 4? In that case an error will be indicated when the program is run. It is far easier and safer to incorporate the ELSE to specify what is to happen if recordtype is not within the correct range. For example, the simple statement

70 ON recordtype% GOSUB 500,600,200,500   ELSE   PRINT "INVALID RECTYPE"

is better than taking no action if the recordtype is outside the range.

The next example shows the use of ELSE and the subroutines included after the LOGICAL END.

```
2100 ON recordtype% GOSUB 2200,2300
     ELSE PRINT"incorrect data"
2110 PRINT s
2120 END
2200     tl=tl + 1
2210     s=s + tl
2220 RETURN : REM ENTRY AT 2200
2300     t2=t2 + 1
2310     s=s - t2
2320 RETURN : REM ENTRY AT 2300
```

It is possible to have only one statement after ELSE. However, if we want to carry out more than one action we can use either a subroutine or a procedure! An example using a subroutine is

```
2100 ON recordtype% GOSUB 2200,2300
     ELSE GOSUB 2400
.........................
2120 END
2200     tl=tl + 1
2210     s=s + tl
2220 RETURN : REM ENTRY AT 2200
2300     t2=t2 + 1
2310     s=s - t2
2320 RETURN : REM ENTRY AT 2300
2400     PRINT "INCORRECT DATA"
2410     END
2420 RETURN : REM ENTRY AT 2400
```

Note that the RETURN on line 2420 is never met.

7.8 The Zero Case in FOR Loops
It was found necessary in chapter 5 to introduce an IF where we wished to code a FOR loop that was sometimes not executed at all. There we used IF and GOTO. A neater way to overcome this problem is to use a procedure or a subroutine. That is, enclose the FOR loop in a procedure or a subroutine and call it when necessary. For example, using a procedure

```
420 IF (start - end ) * gap <= 0 THEN PROCforl
.............
.............
500 END
620 DEF PROCforl
630 FOR kount = start TO end STEP gap
640     PRINT kount
650 NEXT kount
699 ENDPROC : REM FROM 620
```

And using a subroutine

```
420 IF (start - end ) * gap <= 0 THEN GOSUB 630
.............
.............
500 END
630 FOR kount = start TO end STEP gap
640    PRINT kount
650 NEXT kount
699 RETURN : REM ENTRY AT 630
```

In both cases, be careful to code the test on the IF correctly. That is, always use the start, finish and increment (decrement) names or values in the same way as is shown above.

7.9 The Zero Case in REPEAT Loops

It was also found necessary in chapter 5 to introduce an IF where we wished to code a REPEAT loop that was sometimes not executed at all. There we used IF and GOTO. A neater way to get over this problem is to use a procedure or a subroutine. That is, enclose the REPEAT loop in a procedure or a subroutine and call it when necessary. For example, using a procedure

```
700 IF NOT (sum >= 1000) THEN PROCrepeatl
.............
.............
800 END
900 DEF PROCrepeatl
910 REPEAT
920    PRINT number
930    sum=sum+number
940    INPUT number
950 UNTIL sum >= 1000
999 ENDPROC : REM FROM 900
```

And using a subroutine

```
700 IF NOT (sum >= 1000) THEN GOSUB 910
.............
.............
800 END
910 REPEAT
920    PRINT number
930    sum=sum+number
940    INPUT number
950 UNTIL sum >= 1000
999 RETURN : REM ENTRY AT 910
```

In both cases be careful to code the test on the IF correctly. That is, always use the NOT and bracket the condition that is used in the UNTIL statement in the same way as is shown above.

7.10 Converting Subroutines to Procedures

To convert a subroutine to a procedure requires only three changes

    Replace RETURN with ENDPROC
    Introduce DEF PROC at the beginning of the module code
    Replace GOSUBs with PROCs

An example of this is shown for the program versions in chapter 6.

7.11 Summary

Subroutines and procedures are very useful in breaking a program up into manageable, understandable parts. Procedures are preferable since there is no possibility. of specifying an incorrect line number and the procedure has a name. Machines other than the BBC micro often do not have procedures, and subroutines must therefore be used when available.

When using the IF statement, the procedure or subroutine is useful where the action to be carried out is itself a selection or iteration, or where the actions to be carried out would exceed the maximum line length.

When using the ON statement, the subroutine is useful to avoid the necessity of using GOTO (and therefore line numbers) to transfer control to and from the sequence of code required. However, it is still necessary to quote the correct line number on the GOSUB and to remember to put a RETURN at the end of the sequence of code required.

When using the FOR or REPEAT statements the procedure or subroutine is useful in cases where it is required to cater for possible zero iterations.

8 Testing BASIC Programs

8.1 Introduction

Before I consider the topic of testing and debugging, it would be a good idea to look again at the question

"What is a good program?"

and also at the suggested answers:

(1) For a manager

"A program that does what I want it to do".

(2) For a user

"One that's nice and easy to use" (that is user-friendly!).

(3) For a programmer

"One that works".

Testing is the checking of two aspects - that the coding matches the design and that it meets the specification. The first aspect is the concern of the programmer (and generally includes some debugging), the second is the concern of the programmer, user and manager. Sometimes the user or manager has merely an explanation of what the program does rather than a comprehensive specification.

8.2 Programming - Checking that the Coding Matches the Design

Anyone who has coded and tested a program will know that it is impossible to test every single path (sequence of instructions) through a program. However, where the program has been designed in a structured manner and coded using a consistent method of implementing the structure, two benefits should occur. Fewer mistakes should be made in the first place, and secondly the testing can be made more systematic.

Where a program has been structured it is possible to ensure that each instruction is executed at least once during testing. For instance, for a selection it is possible to establish the number of legs that the selection has and to ensure that each leg is used at least once; for an iteration we can ensure that we test "COUNT" loops for a fixed number of times, for different values in the start, stop and gap variables (including the zero case if it can happen), and go through WHILE loops zero times, once and many times.

Where a program has also been modularised (using subroutines or procedures) it is possible to test each module individually and then put the modules together. For example, suppose that we have two modules. We can first test using

```
module1 call
END
module1 code
```

then

```
module2 call
END
module2 code
```

and then merge these to give

```
module1 call
module2 call
END
module1 code
module2 code
```

When an error is found that is merely a coding error (that is, when translating from design into code), the code can be amended and re-tested. This means re-checking some previous correct runs as well as the run that highlighted the error.

When an error is found that is obviously a design error, go back to the design, amend it, re-write the portion of code and re-test.

Two features that can help when debugging are the STOP statement and the PRINT statement.

The STOP statement interrupts a program that is running and indicates the line at which it stopped. It is useful when the actual path taken through the program cannot be determined - to see if a particular portion of code is entered, or in association with the PRINT statement or command to check the values in variables before the program continues. The program run can be continued using the GOTO command (provided that you are not inside a loop) until another STOP or END is reached.

For example, if the following portion of a program is run, the program will halt at 1108 and can be re-started by the command GOTO 1200. The PRINT statement at 1105 can be omitted and then typed as a command when the program halts, if desired. You can change the contents of any variable at this point and then continue with the program, but I would strongly discourage this.

```
 800 sum=0
 900 INPUT number
1100 sum=sum + number
1105 PRINT "sum =",sum," number =",number
1108 STOP
1200 INPUT number
```

Note that the following code will still produce a halt at 1108 and can be re-started, but the program will fail at 1300 because we stopped in the middle of a loop.

```
 800 sum=0
 900 INPUT number
1000 REPEAT
1100   sum=sum + number
1105   PRINT "sum =",sum," number =",number
1108   STOP
1200   INPUT number
1300 UNTIL sum > 200
```

The TRACE facility may also be useful in establishing the path taken through a program for a particular test.

Documenting the results of tests has a two-fold benefit. It ensures that the quality of the testing data can be examined, and it provides a base for testing when amendments are made to the program.

8.3 Programming – Checking that the Coding Meets the Specification

Generally, the programmer will have reconciled his design with the specification before he commences coding; and having checked the coding with the design he should now find that the coding matches the specification.

However, there are two areas that cannot be verified until the coding has been fully tested: the speed at which the program runs and its memory size. If the program runs too slowly, it is possible to improve the speed by changing the BASIC code, although this may reduce the readability of programs in some respects (for example, omission of the REMS and use of the variables A% to Z%). However, to improve speed or to reduce memory size, in some cases it may be necessary to use assembly language. A discussion of assembly language is not possible here, except to state that there is no reason why top-down design cannot be used for the assembly language part and procedures used to "wrap" the assembly language portions.

8.4 User and Manager - Testing

Testing as far as the user and manager are concerned is really evaluation - does this program do what I want it to do?

Obviously there is a difference between testing a purpose-built program and testing one that might possibly be useful. But in both cases the purpose of testing is to ensure that the program caters satisfactorily for all expected (correct) situations and also for anticipated (incorrect) situations. This means that the robustness of the program is being tested. Documenting the results of tests is still necessary to ensure that all appropriate tests are carried out.

To illustrate, suppose that you are testing an education program which asks for pupils´ names. If the specification (explanation) does not tell you, it is necessary to find out the maximum length of name permitted or at least to test the longest name that you currently want to use. Do not forget to note down the answer you obtain, or next time you could get caught out if a longer name comes up.

Even if you know nothing about programming and this is the only section of this book that you have read, remember that computers like to make true/false decisions. So, test all occurrences in your program where you are given a choice (between two or more alternatives) or are given the option of repetition or not; that is, try each of the alternatives and try repetition 0, 1 and more times.

8.5 Summary

No program can be fully tested. But a program that is well designed, consistently coded and adequately tested with sufficient detail for implementation can be regarded as a good program.

9 File Handling

9.1 Introduction

So far, the only method of entering data into a program has been by use of the INPUT statement (see section 2.3) or the READ statement (see section 2.8). Using INPUT the user may enter a number or character string, but the option exists of amending it up until the time he presses the RETURN key. The only method of returning information to the user has been by use of the PRINT statement (see section 2.4).

Where data can be entered by the user, it is also necessary to validate this data. In some cases it is satisfactory to check for certain replies, and only to take default action otherwise. In other cases it is more appropriate to ask the user to re-input the data - each case must be looked at individually and carefully.

9.2 The INKEY and INKEY$ Statements

Sometimes we do not want the user to type a number or string, we merely want one key depressed. We may not even be interested in which key it is; for example, when we want the user to read something on the screen before the program continues.

INKEY and INKEY$ both wait up to a specified time for a key to be depressed; -1 is returned if no key is pressed in the specified time, otherwise INKEY returns the ASCII value and INKEY$ the character pressed.

It is quite easy to construct a loop that waits for the user to press a key. Here is an example that displays some information and asks the user to press any key when he has read it; the program then continues.

```
2210 PRINT word$;" IS THE COLOUR OF ";mean$
2215 PRINT "press any key"
2220 REPEAT:nl=INKEY(100):UNTIL nl <> -1
```

9.3 The DATA, READ and RESTORE Statements

In many programs the data required (or at least some of it) is the same each time that the program is run, therefore we do not want the user to have to type in this data at all.

The DATA statement is used to list such data within the program. It is sensible to include the data in a logical place, either before or after the logical code.

115

The READ statement is used to transfer the data values from the list into the appropriate variables at the desired point.

The RESTORE statement is used to change the position within the data list from which the next data item is taken.

For instance, the following program has 20 items of data which have been listed after the logical end of the program. They have been grouped into 10 lines, each of 2 items for convenience. They represent the data for 4 x 2 items of information and 6 questions (which must have answers), that is, 6 x 2 further items.

The first READ statement encountered (on line 2200) will read the first 2 items from the data list (starting at 5000) into word$ and mean$ (RED and FIRE respectively). Because this READ statement is in a loop (line 2100 - loop from 1 TO 4) the next 6 (3 x 2) items will also be read in at the appropriate time. The data pointer will then be at 7000. But we want to display this 4 x 2 information twice, so a RESTORE statement is required at 2350 to position us back to the beginning of the data, and also at 2500 to re-position us for the 6 x 2 question and answer data.

```
1000 PRINT "I AM GOING TO TEACH YOU THE COLOUR OF
     4 ITEMS"
1100 PRINT "I WILL DEFINE THEM TWICE"
1200 PRINT "THEN I WILL CHECK THEM"
2000 FOR count1=1 TO 2
2100  FOR count2=1 TO 4
2150   CLS
2200   READ word$,mean$
2210   PRINT word$;" IS THE COLOUR OF ";mean$
2215   PRINT "press any key"
2220   REPEAT:nl=INKEY(100):UNTIL nl <> -1
2300  NEXT count2
2350  RESTORE 5000
2400 NEXT count1
2500 RESTORE 7000
3000 FOR count1=1 TO 6
3050  CLS
3100  READ mean$,word$
3110  PRINT "THE COLOUR OF ";mean$;" IS "
3120  INPUT ans$
3130  IF ans$=word$ THEN PRINT "CORRECT"
     ELSE PRINT word$
3150  PRINT "press any key"
3160  REPEAT:nl=INKEY(100):UNTIL nl <> -1
3200 NEXT count1
4000 END
```

```
5000 DATA "RED","FIRE"
5100 DATA "GREEN","GRASS"
5200 DATA "BLUE" ,"SKY"
5300 DATA "YELLOW","SUN"
7000 DATA "SKY","BLUE"
7100 DATA "GRASS","GREEN"
7200 DATA "SUN","YELLOW"
7300 DATA "GRASS","GREEN"
7400 DATA "FIRE","RED"
7500 DATA "SUN","YELLOW"
```

The same program can be used with different data merely by changing the DATA statements. Several versions of the same program, each with the same program code but different data, can easily be produced and stored under different program names.

9.4 Cassette Tape and Diskette Files
A more flexible approach is to store the program and its data separately, either on cassette or diskette. It is then also possible for one program to pass data to another by storing its output on cassette or diskette.

I do not propose to discuss the instructions here in detail. However, to put information on to tape or diskette, it is necessary to open a file for output (OPENOUT), to write out the data (PRINT# or BPUT#) and to close the file (CLOSE#). To get data back from a tape or diskette, it is necessary to open a file for input (OPENIN),to read in the data (INPUT# or BGET#), to test for end of file (EOF#) and to close the file (CLOSE#).

9.5 Printer Files
The words and numbers that would normally be sent to the screen (by PRINT) can be sent as well, or instead, to a line printer. The normal PRINT instruction is retained in the program code (that is, no changes are required to produce text on paper).

Depending on the particular printer that is connected, a series of commands is necessary before the program is run to force output to the printer as well as, or instead of, the screen.

9.6 Summary
It is essential to look at each program individually to decide whether the data is stored with the program or on tape or diskette. For data entered by the user, it is necessary to decide between individual key depression or a number/string terminated by RETURN.

10 Additional Features

10.1 Introduction

BBC BASIC has a number of features - principally graphics, sound and functions - not described elsewhere in this book.

I would always put any graphics or sound code into procedures, for two reasons. Firstly, it is easier to test small modules and then group them together; secondly, if the program is to be transferred to a different microcomputer, which almost certainly has different graphics features, the machine-dependent code is already isolated.

However, it may be necessary to combine several graphics procedures into one procedure after testing individually, because the program runs too slowly, or to change some procedures into assembly language to improve speed.

10.2 Graphics

I do not propose to describe here all the graphics features available. It is far better to experiment on the machine itself. But I will illustrate some ideas which make graphics easier for the user and the programmer. Do not forget that the MODEL A has a smaller set of available graphics.

First of all, graphics will be considered from the user's viewpoint. The main problem here is to try to ensure that the screen does not become too cluttered with pictures and text. A second problem can be that too many colours and too much flashing on the screen can make the presentation off-putting rather than attention-seeking. The third problem is to ensure that the user always knows what to do next; this can be achieved by a short message at the bottom of the screen if the options are few, or a "prompt card" which is kept alongside the screen until the user becomes so familiar with the program that he does not need reminding of the available options. I have also seen too many programs that display the "operating instructions" and options at the beginning of the program, sometimes in several screenfuls, rather than giving the user the option of seeing the instructions or not.

Now how about the programmer? I have already suggested that graphics should be contained in procedures, particularly for testing. Another advantage is that the procedure can easily be incorporated into subsequent programs if desired.

Anyone who has produced graphics programs will know that, after the initial experimentation to find out how the graphics instructions (DRAW, PLOT, GCOL, etc.) work, it is desirable to plan the screen layout carefully, and to use a grid for text and graphics and a separate grid for one's own special characters (VDU 23). For example, figure 10.1 shows a grid for text and graphics, while figure 10.2 depicts a grid for special characters.

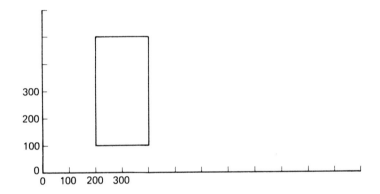

Figure 10.1

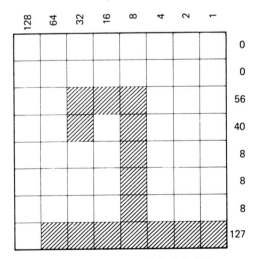

VDU 23, 224, 0, 0, 56, 40, 8, 8, 8, 127

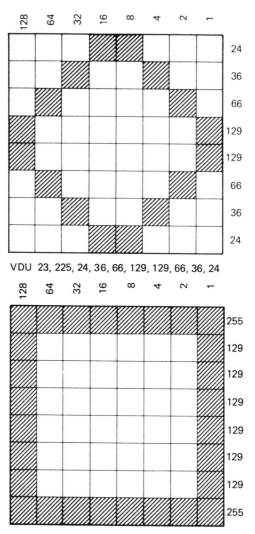

VDU 23, 225, 24, 36, 66, 129, 129, 66, 36, 24

VDU 23, 226, 255, 129, 129, 129, 129, 129, 129, 255

Figure 10.2

I also find it useful when drawing a shape to number the "sides" as it is drawn, so that if I make a mistake I can find the offending code easily. See figure 10.3.

Some of the graphics instructions are not very meaningful and a REM statement will make the program easier to read. But do not forget that they slow the program down, so incorporate them initially and then take them out if you wish to improve the speed of the program. Examples of REM statements are

```
COLOUR 129 : REM red text background
GCOL 0,130 : REM yellow graphics background
```

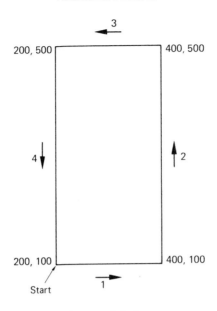

Figure 10.3

Readers who would like to explore in depth the graphics features of the BBC micro are recommended to read "Advanced Graphics with the BBC Microcomputer", by I.O. Angell and B.J. Jones (Macmillan, 1983).

10.3 Sound
I do not propose to describe here the sound features available. It is far better to experiment on the machine itself. But I will illustrate two ideas that make sound features easier for the programmer to use. I have already suggested that sound should be contained in procedures, particularly for testing. Another advantage is that the procedure can easily be incorporated into subsequent programs if desired.

As with graphics, it is necessary to plan the sounds required. The instructions (SOUND and ENVELOPE) are not particularly meaningful; documentation describing the sound in musical as well as in program terms is desirable, either as comments (REM) in the program itself or as separate manual documentation. For example

```
SOUND 1,-15,53,20 : REM channel 1,loudest,middle
c,one second
```

Once again, those readers who would like to go more deeply into the sound features of the BBC micro are advised to read "Using Sound and Speech on the BBC Microcomputer" by M. Phillips (Macmillan, 1984).

10.4 Functions

BBC BASIC has a number of functions which can easily be used, such as SQR, COS, etc., but there is a useful feature that enables you to define a new function. This is illustrated in the next example.

```
 5 number%=2 : power%=3
10 PRINT FNpower(number%,power%)
20 END
30 DEF FNpower(pnumber%,ppower%)
40 LOCAL result%,count%
50   result% =1
60   FOR count% = 1 TO ppower%
70     result% =result% * pnumber%
80   NEXT count%
90 = result%
```

Lines 30 to 90 define (DEF) a function (FN) with the name FNpower. A function always has a name (line 30) and an answer (line 90). The LOCAL (line 40) merely indicates that result% and count% are local to this function and thus there will be no problems if the same names are used for other purposes outside the function.

This function, in lines 50 to 80, calculates the result of raising an integer to a positive (>=1) power in result%. This variable name is therefore used to pass the answer back on line 90 using the = sign. Notice that the function has been placed after END, so that there is no possibility of executing the code except by calling the function (line 10 above). The function could be placed at the beginning, provided that there is a jump over it to the first executable instruction (that is, functions are always placed out-of-line).

Note that BBC BASIC has a power operator which can be used in any expression. The example given is merely to illustrate the function facility.

Functions can be used to calculate a numeric or string result. For example, the following function returns the last character of a character string.

```
100 DEF FNlast(string$)
110 LOCAL length
120 length=LEN(string$)
140 =MID$(string$,length,1)
```

10.5 Summary

The sections in this chapter offer a few hints on how to make good use of graphics, sound and functions in writing good programs.

11   Implementation and Review

11.1 Introduction
Implementation is the introduction of the program into the application area, such as a classroom, office or home. Review is the evaluation of the program's performance.

11.2 General Implementation
For new users and/or managers, one of the first problems may be the organisation of the suite of programs.

For programs on tape I would recommend a manual index for each tape, showing the start position for each program. When using tape or diskette I would also recommend making copies of each program for everyday use, retaining the original master from which to make further copies as necessary. Some users will also be more confident in using the computer if the tapes and diskettes cannot be over-written (assuming it is not necessary to store data files on the same tape or diskette!). When updating programs do not forget to update all the copies.

Implementation is generally carried out in at least two stages: the program is implemented in a small area and, after review, implemented as desired.

Documenting the effects of implementation ensure that urgent corrections can be distinguished from desirable alterations.

11.3 Individual Aids for Implementation
Obviously, all users will need some training and practice in using the keyboard and possibly also the tape, diskette, printer, etc. But for each individual program there is generally a set of operating instructions which will become more familiar only as the program is repeatedly used. Many programs explain these operations at the beginning of the program and/or in the written explanation, but I have found it more useful to provide users with "prompt cards" which highlight the actions needed to carry out specific

123

operations, particularly where graphics are used. For example

Action	Key
Stop program	S
End program	E
Move to next section	N
Repeat this section	R

These cards can be dispensed with, once the user has become familiar with the operation of the program. Some programs are able to provide this facility with a continuous "MENU" on part of the screen, but generally there is insufficient room.

In many instances it may be necessary to produce user forms which must be completed before data can be entered into the program. The layout for these may be suggested in the written explanation, but alternatively you may have to invent your own. For instance, you may have a program which produces league tables although the written explanation does not suggest how you should collate your data before starting to run the program.

11.4 Review
There is obviously a difference between reviewing a purpose-built program and an existing one that might be useful.

Documenting the comments made by manager, user and programmer during review ensures that due care is taken before amendments are made, or the program is accepted or rejected as appropriate.

11.5 Summary
Implementation must be thoroughly prepared for it to be successful. However, a good program will have sufficient detail in its explanation (including operating instructions) to enable implementation to be smoothly carried out.

12   Summary

12.1 The Programmer

This book is principally for programmers and therefore I shall extract here a list of points which act as an aide-memoire when producing programs.

(1) Remember the user at all times, and include sufficient data validation.
(2) Complete the design properly before coding, and if errors are found go back and amend the design (if necessary) before changing the code.
(3) Use the same names in design and coding and keep a list outside the program code.
(4) Code from design in a structured, consistent fashion.
(5) Code and test in a systematic way.
(6) When implementing structure in code, I prefer procedures to subroutines and subroutines to GOTOs. If you have to use GOTO use it properly, as in the examples in this book. Do not forget to cater for the zero case in loops where necessary.
(7) Do not clutter outputs, but do give users the option of seeing the operating instructions if they so wish.
(8) Keep adequate documentation, such as specification, design (including variable name list), up-to-date program listing, test results, operating instructions, prompt cards and planning grids. Then when you have to change the program, amend for a different machine or extract parts for a different program, all the information is available!

12.2 The Manager

The most important point for the manager is to ensure that the program does meet the specification where purpose-built, or at least that it is of genuine assistance. He should not assume that any part of the program works unless it has been successfully tested.

12.3 The User

The above point applies also to the user, but since the user has more direct contact with a program when implemented, he should not be afraid to request a better program or to suggest that there is something fundamentally wrong with a program.

12.4 Summary

Producing programs for the BBC micro can be fun and very rewarding if due attention is paid to specification, design, coding, testing, implementation and review.

Index*